IMPULSE

Biologynary

Biologyanry is Made of two Words i.e. Biology + Dictionary. Dictionaries teach the correct spellings, pronunciation and meanings of the words through which learner's knowledge of varied terms, definitions, principles, methods & theorems, etc. enhances.

The Biologynary has been designed to deal precisely with those topics, which students of schools and colleges and aspirants of various competitive examinations like NEET & Other Medical Entrances are always looking for. To the point and concise information has been provided in this. This dictionary covers the terms, definitions, concepts, methods & laws starting from alphabet A to alphabet Z. Plus all the terms of NCERT Textbook have been covered in the dictionary.

-   Keshav Mehta (B.Sc Zoology Hons.)

Entrepreneur, Author

A

Abaxial

The term abaxial (or dorsal) describes a plant part, side or surface facing away from the axis of any organ or part; eccentric.

Abdomen

In vertebrates, the portion of the trunk containing visceral organs other than heart and lungs; in arthropods, the posterior portion of the body made up of similar segments and containing the reproductive organs and part of the digestive tract.

Abiotic

Nonliving; specifically, the nonliving components of an ecosystem, such as temperature, humidity, the mineral content of the soil, etc.

Aboral

Upside down, the aboral surface of a starfish. About away from the mouth in organisms with no distinct front or back sides

Abscisic acid

A plant hormone that generally acts to inhibit growth, promote dormancy, and help the plant tolerate stressful conditions.

Abscission

In plants, the dropping of leaves, flowers, fruits, or stems at the end of a growing season, as the result of the formation of a two-layered zone of specialized cells (the abscission zone) and the action of a hormone.

Absorption

The movement of water and dissolved substances into a cell, tissue, or organism.

Absorption spectrum

The range of a pigment's ability to absorb various wavelengths of light.

Abyssal zone

The portion of the ocean floor where light does not penetrate and where temperatures are cold and pressures intense.

Acanthocephala

The spiny-headed worms, a phylum of helminths; adults are parasitic in the alimentary canal of vertebrates.

Accessory cells

Any nonlymphocytic cell that helps in the induction of the immune response by presenting antigen to a helper T lymphocyte.

Acoelomates

An animal that lacks a coelom. Acoelomates, which include the flatworm, fluke, tapeworm, and ribbon worm, exhibit bilateral symmetry and possess one internal space, the digestive cavity.

Acclimatization

Physiological adjustment to a change in an environmental factor.

Accommodation

The automatic adjustment of an eye to focus on near objects.

Acellular

Containing no cells; not made of cells.

Accessory Cell

A cell which is associated with the guard *cell* of a stoma

Acetylcholine

One of the most common neurotransmitters; functions by binding to receptors and altering the permeability of the postsynaptic membrane to specific ions, either depolarizing or hyperpolarizing the membrane.

Acetyl CoA

The entry compound for the Krebs cycle in cellular respiration; formed from a fragment of pyruvate attached to a coenzyme.

Achlamydeous

Not having a floral envelope or perianth.

Acid

A substance that increases the hydrogen ion concentration in a solution

.Acid precipitation

Rain, snow, or fog that is more acidic than pH 5.6.

Acoelomate

A solid-bodied animal lacking a cavity between the gut and outer body wall.

Acrocentric

Having the centromere located near one end of the chromosome so that one chromosomal arm is long and the other is short.

Acrosome

An organelle at the tip of a sperm cell that helps the sperm penetrate the egg.

ACTH

Abbreviation of adrenocorticotropic hormone.

Actin

A globular protein that links into chains, two of which twist helically about each other, forming microfilaments in muscle and other contractile elements in cells.

Actinomorphic

Capable of being divided into equal halves along any diameter, as the flowers of the rose or tulip; radially symmetrical.

Action potential

A rapid change in the membrane potential of an excitable cell, caused by stimulus-triggered, selective opening and closing of voltage-sensitive gates in sodium and potassium ion channels.

Activation energy

The energy that must be possessed by atoms or molecules to react.

Active site

The specific portion of an enzyme that attaches to the substrate using weak chemical bonds.

Active transport

The movement of a substance across a biological membrane against its concentration or electrochemical gradient, with the help of energy input and specific transport proteins.

Adaptation

The evolution of features that make a group of organisms better suited to live and reproduce in their environment.

Adaptive peak

An equilibrium state in a population when the gene pool has allele frequencies that maximize the average fitness of a population's members.

Adaptive radiation

The emergence of numerous species from a common ancestor introduced into an environment, presenting a diversity of new opportunities and problems.

Adenosine diphosphate

A nucleotide consisting of adenine, ribose, and two phosphate groups; formed by the removal of one phosphate from an ATP molecule.

Adenosine monophosphate

A nucleotide consisting of adenine, ribose, and one phosphate group; can be formed by the removal of two phosphates from an ATP molecule; in its cyclic form, functions as a "second messenger" for many vertebrate hormones and neurotransmitters.

Adenosine triphosphate

An adenine-containing nucleoside triphosphate that releases free energy when its phosphate bonds are hydrolyzed. This energy is used to drive endergonic reactions in cells.

Adenylyl cyclase

An enzyme that converts ATP to cyclic AMP in response to a chemical signal.

ADH

Abbreviation of antidiuretic hormone.

Adhesion

The tendency of different kinds of molecules to stick together.

ADP

Abbreviation of adenosine diphosphate.

Adaxial

In botany terminology, adaxial describes a side or surface nearest or facing toward the axis of an organ or organism, such as the upper surface of a leaf lamina

Adipocytes

Any of various cells found in adipose tissue that is specialized for the storage of fat. Also called *adipocyte.*

Adnate

Unlike parts or organs; growing closely attached

Adrenal gland

An endocrine gland located adjacent to the kidney in mammals; composed of two glandular portions: an outer cortex, which response to endocrine signals in reacting to stress and effecting salt and water balance, and a central medulla, which response to nervous inputs resulting from stress.

Adrenaline

A hormone, produced by the medulla of the adrenal gland, that increases the concentration of glucose in the blood, raises blood pressure and heartbeat rate, and increases muscular power and resistance to fatigue; also a neurotransmitter across synaptic junctions. Also called epinephrine.

Adrenocorticotropic hormone (ACTH)

A hormone, produced by the anterior lobe of the pituitary gland, that stimulates the production of cortisol by the adrenal cortex.

Adventitious

Referring to a structure arising from an unusual place, such as roots growing from stems or leaves.

Aerenchyma

A spongy tissue with large air spaces found between the cells of the stems and leaves of aquatic plants, providing buoyancy and allowing the circulation of gases.

Aerobic

Containing oxygen; referring to an organism, environment, or cellular process that requires oxygen.

Aerial

Existing or living in the air.

Aestivation

Cessation from or slowing of activity during the summer; especially slowing of metabolism in some animals

Afferent

Bringing inward to a central part, applied to nerves and blood vessels.

Agar

A gelatinous material prepared from certain red algae that are used to solidify nutrient media for growing microorganisms.

Age structure

The relative number of individuals of each age in a population.

Agnathan

A member of a jawless class of vertebrates represented today by the lampreys and hagfishes.

Agonistic behaviour

A type of behaviour involving a contest of some kind that determines which competitor gains access to some resource, such as food or mates.

Alburnum

The outer zone of wood in a tree, next to the bark. Sapwood is generally lighter than heartwood.

AIDS (acquired immunodeficiency syndrome)

The name of the late stages of HIV infection; defined by a specified reduction of T cells and the appearance of characteristic secondary infections.

Air sacs

An air-filled space in the body of a bird that forms a connection between the lungs and bone cavities and aids in breathing and temperature regulation.

Aldehyde

An organic molecule with a carbonyl group located at the end of the carbon skeleton.

Aldosterone

An adrenal hormone that acts on the distal tubules of the kidney to stimulate the reabsorption of sodium (Na^+) and the passive flow of water from the filtrate.

Aleurone layer

The outermost cell layer of the endosperm of the grains (seeds) of wheat and other grasses; when acted upon by gibberellin, the aleurone layer releases enzymes that digest the stored food of the endosperm into small nutrient molecules that can be taken up by the embryo.

Algae

A photosynthetic, plantlike protist.

Alligator

Either of two large reptiles, *Alligator mississipiensis* of the southeast United States or *A. Sinensis* of China, having sharp teeth and powerful jaws. They differ from crocodiles in having a broader, shorter snout.

Alimentary canal

The tube or passage of the digestive system through which food passes, nutrients are absorbed, waste is eliminated.

Alkalinity

pH values above 7.

Alkaline

About substances that increase the relative number of hydroxide ions (OH^-) in a solution; having a pH greater than 7; basic; opposite of acidic.

Alkaloids

A type of chemical commonly found in plants and often having medicinal properties. e.g.: atropine, caffeine, morphine, nicotine, quinine.

All-or-none event

An action that occurs either completely or not at all, such as the generation of an action potential by a neuron.

Allantois

One of four extraembryonic membranes; serves as a repository for the embryo's nitrogenous waste.

Allele

An alternative form of a gene.

Allele frequency

The proportion of a particular allele in a population.

Allergic reaction

An inflammatory response triggered by a weak antigen (an allergen) to which most individuals do not react; involves the release of large amounts of histamine from mast cells.

Allometric growth

The variation in the relative rates of growth of various parts of the body, which helps shape the organism.

Allopatric speciation

A mode of speciation induced when the ancestral population becomes segregated by a geographical barrier.

Allopolyploid

A common type of polyploid species resulting from two different species interbreeding and combining their chromosomes.

Allosteric site

A specific receptor site on an enzyme molecule remote from the active site. Molecules bind to the allosteric site and change the shape of the active site, making it either more or less receptive to the substrate.

Allozymes

Slightly different versions of the same enzyme, distinguishable via gel electrophoresis.

Alpha helix

A spiral shape constituting one form of the secondary structure of proteins, arising from a specific hydrogen-bonding structure.

Alternation of generations

A life cycle in which there is both a multicellular diploid form, the sporophyte, and a multicellular haploid form, the gametophyte; characteristic of plants.

Alternative splicing

In alternative splicing, the same pre-mRNA molecule, which consists of introns and exons, is spliced in different ways to produce mature mRNAs of different lengths and different functionality.

Altruistic behaviour

The aiding of another individual at one's own risk or expense.

Alveolus

One of the dead-end, multilobed air sacs that constitute the gas exchange surface of the lungs. Or One of the milk-secreting sacs of epithelial tissue in the mammary glands.

Amino acids

An organic molecule possessing both carboxyl and amino groups. Amino acids serve as the monomers of proteins.

Amino group

A functional group that consists of a nitrogen atom bonded to two hydrogen atoms; can act as a base in solution, accepting a hydrogen ion and acquiring a charge of $+1$.

Aminoacyl

A family of enzymes, at least one for each amino acid, that catalyzes the attachment of an amino acid to its specific tRNA molecule.

Amitosis

Direct cell division, that is, the cell divides by simple cleavage of the nucleus without the formation of supreme spindle figures or chromosomes.

Ammonification

The process by which decomposers break down proteins and amino acids, releasing the excess nitrogen in the form of ammonia (NH_3) or ammonium ion (NH_4^+).

Amniocentesis

A technique for determining genetic abnormalities in a fetus by the presence of certain chemicals or defective fetal cells in the amniotic fluid, obtained by aspiration from a needle inserted into the uterus.

Amnion

The innermost of four extraembryonic membranes; encloses a fluid-filled sac in which the embryo is suspended.

Amniote

A vertebrate possessing an amnion surrounding the embryo; reptiles, birds, and mammals are amniotes.

Amniotic egg

A shelled, water-retaining egg that enables reptiles, birds, and egg-laying mammals to complete their life cycles on dry land.

Amoeboid

Moving or feeding using pseudopodia (temporary cytoplasmic protrusions from the cell body).

AMP

Abbreviation of adenosine monophosphate.

Amphibia

The vertebrate class of amphibians, represented by frogs, salamanders, and caecilians.

Amphibious

Living or able to live both land and water.

Amphipathic molecule

A molecule that has both a hydrophilic region and a hydrophobic region.

Amphioxus

Any of various small, flattened marine organisms of the subphylum Cephalochordata, structurally similar to the vertebrates but having a notochord rather than a true vertebral column. Also called *amphioxus*.

Amphoteric

Having the characteristics of an acid and a base and capable of reacting chemically either as an acid or a base.

Amphistomatic

Of a leaf, Having stomata on both surfaces

Amylopectin

The outer portion of a starch granule consisting of insoluble, highly branched polysaccharides of high molecular weight.

Amyloplasts/ starch plastids

Amyloplasts are non-pigmented organelles found in plant cells responsible for the storage of amylopectin, a form of starch, through the polymerization of glucose. Amyloplasts also convert this starch into sugar, for when the plant needs energy.

Anabolic steroids

Synthetic chemical variants of the male sex hormone testosterone; they produce increased muscle mass but also suppress testosterone production, leading to shrinkage of the testes, growth of the breasts, and premature baldness; long-term use increases the risk of kidney and liver damage and liver cancer.

Anabolism

Within a cell or organism, the sum of all biosynthetic reactions (that is, chemical reactions in which larger molecules are formed from smaller ones).

Anaerobic

Lacking oxygen; referring to an organism, environment, or cellular process that lacks oxygen and maybe poisoned by it.

Anagenesis

A pattern of evolutionary change involving the transformation of an entire population, sometimes to a state different enough from the ancestral population to justify renaming it as a separate species; also called phyletic evolution.

Analogy

The similarity of structure between two species that are not closely related; attributable to convergent evolution.

Analogous

Applied to structures similar in function but different in evolutionary origins, such as the wing of a bird and the wing of an insect.

Anaphase

The third stage of mitosis, beginning when the centromeres of duplicated chromosomes divide and sister chromatids separate from each other, and ending when a complete set of daughter chromosomes are located at each of the two poles of the cell.

Anatomy

The morphological structure of a plant or an animal or of any of its parts.

Androecium

The male reproductive organs of a flower considered as a group; the stamens. Compare gynoecium.

Androgen

The principal male steroid hormones, such as testosterone, which stimulate the development and maintenance of the male reproductive system and secondary sex characteristics.

Aneuploidy

A chromosomal aberration in which certain chromosomes are present in extra copies or are deficient in number.

Angiosperms

A flowering plant, which forms seeds inside a protective chamber called an ovary.

Animalia

Animals are a major group of multicellular organisms, of the kingdom Animalia or metazoa.

Animal starch

One form in which body is fuel is stored; stored primarily in the liver and broken down into glucose when needed by the body.

Anisogamous

A union between two gametes that differ in the size of the form.

Anion

A negatively charged ion.

Anklebones

The bone in the ankle that articulates with the leg bones to form the ankle joint

Annual

A plant that completes its entire life cycle in a single year or growing season.

Antennae

Long, paired sensory appendages on the head of many arthropods.

Anterior

Referring to the head end of a bilaterally symmetrical animal.

Anther

The terminal pollen sac of a stamen, inside which pollen grains with male gametes form in the flower of an angiosperm.

Antheridium

In plants, the male gametangium, a moist chamber in which gametes develop.

Anthocyanin

Natural water-soluble pigments of blue, purple or red which are dissolved in the cell sap vacuole of plant cells.

Anthropoid

A higher primate; includes monkeys, apes, and humans.

Antibiotic

A chemical that kills bacteria or inhibits their growth.

Antibiotic resistance

Antibiotic resistance is the ability of a microorganism to withstand the effects of an antibiotic. It is a specific type of drug resistance.

Antibody

An antigen-binding immunoglobulin, produced by B cells, that functions as the effector in an immune response.

Anticodon

A specialized base triplet on one end of a tRNA molecule that recognizes a particular complementary codon on an mRNA molecule.

Antidiuretic hormone (ADH)

A hormone is important in osmoregulation.

Antigen

A foreign macromolecule that does not belong to the host organism and that elicits an immune response.

Anus

The opening at the lower end of the digestive tract through which solid waste is excreted.

Anurans

Any of numerous tailless, aquatic, semiaquatic, or terrestrial amphibians of the order Anura and especially of the family Ranidae, characteristically having a smooth moist skin, webbed feet, and long hind legs adapted for leaping.

Aorta

The major artery in blood-circulating systems; the aorta sends blood to the other body tissues.

Appendicular

Elating to, or consisting of an appendage or appendages, especially the limbs: the appendicular skeleton.

Aphotic zone

The part of the ocean beneath the photic zone, where light does not penetrate sufficiently for photosynthesis to occur.

Apical dominance

The concentration of growth at the tip of a plant shoot, where a terminal bud partially inhibits axillary bud growth.

Apical meristem

Embryonic plant tissue in the tips of roots and in the buds of shoots that supplies cells for the plant to grow in length.

Apocarpous

Consisting of carpels that are free from one another as in buttercups or roses.

Apomorphic character

A derived phenotypic character, or homology, that evolved after a branch diverged from a phylogenetic tree.

Apoplast

In plants, the nonliving continuum formed by the extracellular pathway provided by the continuous matrix of cell walls.

Apoptosis

Programmed cell death brought about by signals that trigger the activation of a cascade of "suicide" proteins in the cells destined to die.

Aposematic colouration

The bright colouration of animals with effective physical or chemical defences that acts as a warning to predators.

Aquaporin

A transport protein in the plasma membranes of a plant or animal cell that specifically facilitates the diffusion of water across the membrane (osmosis).

Aquatic

Consisting of, relating to, or being in water; *an aquatic environment.*

Aqueous solution

A solution in which water is the solvent.

Arboreal

Tree-dwelling.

Archaea

One of two prokaryotic domains, the other being the Bacteria.

Arches

Arches are curved structures, arch-like in profile, which span the foot.

Archenteron

The central cavity of the gastrula, which ultimately becomes the intestinal or digestive cavity.

Archegonium

In plants, the female gametangium, a moist chamber in which gametes develop.

Archenteron

The endoderm-lined cavity, formed during the gastrulation process, that develops into the digestive tract of an animal.

Archezoa

The primitive eukaryotic group that includes diplomonads, such as Giardia; some systematists assign kingdom status to archezoans.

Arteriole

A very small artery. See also artery.

Arteries

Arteries are blood vessels that carry blood away from the heart

Artery

A vessel that carries blood away from the heart to organs throughout the body.

Arteriosclerosis

A cardiovascular disease caused by the formation of hard plaques within the arteries.

Artificial selection

The selective breeding of domesticated plants and animals to encourage the occurrence of desirable traits.

Ascus

A saclike spore capsule located at the tip of the ascocarp in dikaryotic hyphae; defining feature of the Ascomycota division of fungi.

Asexual reproduction

A type of reproduction involving only one parent that produces genetically identical offspring by budding or by the division of a single cell or the entire organism into two or more parts.

Aschelminth

The Aschelminthes (also known as Aeschelminthes, Nemathelminthes, or Pseudocoelomata), closely associated with the Platyhelminthes, are an obsolete phylum of pseudocoelomate and other similar animals that are no longer considered closely related and have been promoted to phyla in their own right.

Assimilation

The energy-requiring process by which plant cells convert nitrate ions (NO_3^-) taken up by the roots of plants into ammonium ions (NH_4^+), which can then be used in the synthesis of amino acids and other nitrogenous compounds.

Associative learning

The acquired ability to associate one stimulus with another; also called classical conditioning.

Assortative mating

A type of nonrandom mating in which mating partners resemble each other in certain phenotypic characters.

Astragalus

The bone of the ankle which articulates with the bones of the leg. Also known as talus.

Astrocytes

A star-shaped cell, especially a neuroglial cell of nervous tissue.

Asymmetrical

Irregular in shape or outline.

Asymmetric carbon

A carbon atom covalently bonded to four different atoms or groups of atoms.

Atactostele

A type of monocotyledonous siphonostele in which the vascular bundles are dispersed irregularly throughout the centre of the stem.

Atmospheric pressure

The weight of the Earth's atmosphere over a unit area of the Earth's surface.

Atom

The smallest unit of matter that retains the properties of an element.

Atomic mass

The mass of an atom of a chemical element expressed in atomic mass units.

Atomic number

The number of protons in the nucleus of an atom, unique for each element and designated by a subscript to the left of the elemental symbol.

Atomic Theory

The physical theory of the structure, properties, and behaviour of the atom.

Atomic weight

The total atomic mass, which is the mass in grams of one mole of the atom.

ATP

Abbreviation of adenosine triphosphate, the principal energy-carrying compound of the cell.

ATP Synthase

A cluster of several membrane proteins found in the mitochondrial cristae (and bacterial plasma membrane) that function in chemiosmosis with adjacent electron transport chains, using the energy of a hydrogen-ion concentration gradient to make ATP. ATP synthases provide a port through which hydrogen ions diffuse into the matrix of a mitochondrion.

Atrioventricular node

A group of slow-conducting fibres in the atrium of the vertebrate heart that is stimulated by impulses originating in the sinoatrial node (the pacemaker) and that conduct impulses to the bundle of His, a group of fibres that stimulate contraction of the ventricles.

Atrioventricular valve

A valve in the heart between each atrium and ventricle that prevents a backflow of blood when the ventricles contract.

Atrium

A chamber that receives blood returning to the vertebrate heart.

Auricles

The flap of the ear in the form of a funnel-like organ which collects the sound waves. Called also pinna.

Autocatalysis

A single chemical reaction is said to have undergone autocatalysis, or be autocatalytic if the reaction product is itself the catalyst for that reaction.

Autoecious

Having all stages of a life cycle occurring on the same host. Eg.; fungi

Autogenesis model

According to this model, eukaryotic cells evolved by the specialization of internal membranes originally derived from prokaryotic plasma membranes.

Autoimmune disease

An immunological disorder in which the immune system turns against itself.

Autonomic nervous system

A subdivision of the motor nervous system of vertebrates that regulates the internal environment; consists of the sympathetic and parasympathetic divisions.

Autopolyploid

A type of polyploid species resulting from one species doubling its chromosome number to become tetraploid, which may self-fertilize or mate with other tetraploids.

Autosomes

A chromosome that is not directly involved in determining sex, as opposed to the sex chromosomes.

Autotroph

An organism that obtains organic food molecules without eating other organisms. Autotrophs use energy from the sun or from the oxidation of inorganic substances to make organic molecules from inorganic ones.

Autumn wood

The season of the year between summer and winter, lasting from the autumnal equinox to the winter solstice and from September to December in the Northern Hemisphere; fall.

Auxin

A class of plant hormones, including indoleacetic acid (IAA), having a variety of effects, such as phototropic response through the stimulation of cell elongation, stimulation of secondary growth, and the development of leaf traces and fruit.

Auxotroph

A nutritional mutant that is unable to synthesize and that cannot grow on media lacking certain essential molecules normally synthesized by wild-type strains of the same species.

Aves

The vertebrate class of birds, characterized by feathers and other flight adaptations.

Axial

Relating to, characterized by, or forming an axis.

Axile

Situated along the central axis of an ovary having two or more locules.

Axillary buds

An embryonic shoot present in the angle formed by a leaf and stem.

Axial filaments

The central filament of a flagellum or cilium. Also called an *axoneme*.

Axis

An imaginary line passing through a body or organ around which parts are symmetrically aligned.

Axon

A typically long extension, or process, from a neuron that carries nerve impulses away from the cell body toward target cells.

B

B cell

A type of lymphocyte that develops in the bone marrow and later produces antibodies, which mediate humoral immunity.

Bacilli (pl.) Bacillus (Sin.)

aerobic rod-shaped spore-producing bacterium; often occurring in chainlike formations

Bacteria

One of two prokaryotic domains, the other being the Archaea.

Bacteriophage

A virus that parasitizes a bacterial cell.

Bacterium (Sin.) Bacteria (Pl.)

A prokaryotic microorganism in Domain Bacteria.

Balanced polymorphism

A type of polymorphism in which the frequencies of the coexisting forms do not change noticeably over many generations.

Bark

All tissues external to the vascular cambium in a plant growing in thickness, consisting of phloem, phelloderm, cork cambium, and cork.

Barr body

A dense object lying along the inside of the nuclear envelope in female mammalian cells, representing an inactivated X chromosome.

Basal

Located at or near the base of a plant stem, or at the base of any other plant part.

Basal body

A eukaryotic cell organelle consisting of a 9 + 0 arrangement of microtubule triplets; may organize the microtubule assembly of a cilium or flagellum; structurally identical to a centriole.

Basal metabolic rate (BMR)

The minimal number of kilocalories a resting animal requires to fuel itself for a given time.

Base

A substance that reduces the hydrogen ion concentration in a solution.

Basement membrane

The floor of an epithelial membrane on which the basal cells rest.

Base-pair substitution

A point mutation; the replacement of one nucleotide and its partner from the complementary DNA strand by another pair of nucleotides.

Base-pairing principle

In the formation of nucleic acids, the requirement that adenine must always pair with thymine (or uracil) and guanine with cytosine.

Basidium

A reproductive appendage that produces sexual spores on the gills of mushrooms. The fungal division Basidiomycota is named for this structure.

Basifixed

Attached by the base, as certain anthers are to their filaments.

Batesian mimicry

A type of mimicry in which a harmless species looks like a different species that is poisonous or otherwise harmful to predators.

Behaviour

All of the acts an organism performs, as in, for example, seeking a suitable habitat, obtaining food, avoiding predators, and seeking a mate and reproducing.

Behavioural ecology

A heuristic approach based on the expectation that Darwinian fitness (reproductive success) is improved by optimal behaviour.

Benthic zone

The bottom surfaces of aquatic environments.

Benign

Not life-threatening or severe, and likely to respond to treatment, as a tumour that is not malignant.

Biannuals

Occurring twice a year.

Biennial

A plant that requires two years to complete its life cycle.

Bilateral symmetry

Characterizing a body form with a central longitudinal plane that divides the body into two equal but opposite halves.

Bilateria

Members of the branch of eumetazoans possessing bilateral symmetry.

Bile

A yellow secretion of the vertebrate liver, temporarily stored in the gallbladder and composed of organic salts that emulsify fats in the small intestine.

Binary fission

The type of cell division by which prokaryotes reproduce; each dividing daughter cell receives a copy of the single parental chromosome.

Binomial

The two-part Latinized name of a species, consisting of the genus and specific epithet.

Biochemical pathway

An ordered series of chemical reactions in a living cell, in which each step is catalyzed by a specific enzyme; different biochemical pathways serve different functions in the life of the cell.

Biodiversity hotspot

A relatively small area with an exceptional concentration of species.

Bioenergetics

The study of how organisms manage their energy resources.

Biogeochemical cycles

The various nutrient circuits, which involve both biotic and abiotic components of ecosystems.

Biogeography

The study of the past and present distribution of species.

Biological clock

Proposed internal factor(s) in organisms that governs functions that occur rhythmically in the absence of external stimuli.

Biological magnification

Atrophic process in which retained substances become more concentrated with each link in the food chain.

Biologynary

Biological species

A population or group of populations whose members have the potential to interbreed.

Biomass

The dry weight of organic matter comprising a group of organisms in a particular habitat.

Biome

One of the world's major communities, classified according to the predominant vegetation and characterized by adaptations of organisms to that particular environment.

Biosphere

The entire portion of Earth that is inhabited by life; the sum of all the planet's communities and ecosystems.

Biosynthesis

Formation by living organisms of organic compounds from elements or simple compounds.

Biotechnology

The industrial use of living organisms or their components to improve human health and food production.

Biotic

About the living organisms in the environment.

Bipedal

Walking upright on two feet.

Bisexual

Having both male and female reproductive organs; hermaphroditic.

Biting

Causing a stinging sensation; nipping: *biting cold.*

Bivalve
Having a shell consisting of two hinged valves.

Bivalent

A pair of homologous, synapsed chromosomes associated together during meiosis.

Blade

The broad expanded photosynthetic part of the thallus of a multicellular alga or a simple plant.

Blastocoel

The fluid-filled cavity that forms in the centre of the blastula embryo.

Blastocyst

An embryonic stage in mammals; a hollow ball of cells produced one week after fertilization in humans.

Blastodisc

Disklike area on the surface of a large, yolky egg that undergoes cleavage and gives rise to the embryo.

Blastopore

The opening of the archenteron in the gastrula that develops into the mouth in protostomes and the anus in deuterostomes.

Blastula

The hollow ball of cells marking the end stage of cleavage during early embryonic development.

Blood

A type of connective tissue with a fluid matrix called plasma in which blood cells are suspended.

Blood flukes.

A blood fluke species related to Schistosoma haematobium which lives in the blood of host like human

Blood-brain barrier

A specialized capillary arrangement in the brain that restricts the passage of most substances into the brain, thereby preventing dramatic fluctuations in the brain's environment.

Blood pressure

The hydrostatic force that blood exerts against the wall of a vessel.

Blood vascular system

When blood vessels connect to form a region of diffuse vascular supply it is called an anastomosis

Biology

The scientific study of life and living organisms. Botany, zoology, and ecology are all branches of biology.

Bond energy

The quantity of energy that must be absorbed to break a particular kind of chemical bond; equal to the quantity of energy the bond releases when it forms.

Bond strength

The strength with which a chemical bond holds two atoms together; conventionally measured in terms of the amount of energy, in kilocalories per mole, required to break the bond.

Bony

Having an internal skeleton of bones.

Book lungs

Organs of gas exchange in spiders, consisting of stacked plates contained in an internal chamber.

Botany

The study of plants.

Bottleneck effect

Genetic drift resulting from the reduction of a population, typically by a natural disaster, such that the surviving population is no longer genetically representative of the original population.

Bowman's capsule

A cup-shaped receptacle in the vertebrate kidney that is the initial, expanded segment of the nephron where filtrate enters from the blood.

Box

A small portion of a gene or protein that appears in many genes or proteins that are related in the structure; the box usually has some specific function, sometimes called a "motif", like binding DNA or interacting with specific proteins or other molecules.

Brain

The master control centre in an animal; in vertebrates, the brain and spinal cord make up the central nervous system.

Brainstem

The hindbrain and midbrain of the vertebrate central nervous system. In humans, it forms a cap on the anterior end of the spinal cord, extending to about the middle of the brain.

Bracteates

Having bracts.

Bryophyte

The mosses, liverworts, and hornworts; a group of nonvascular plants that inhabit the land but lack many of the terrestrial adaptations of vascular plants.

Bronchus

One of a pair of respiratory tubes branching into either lung at the lower end of the trachea; it subdivides into progressively finer passageways, the bronchioles, culminating in the alveoli.

Bucco-pharyngeal

About the cheek and the pharynx or to the mouth and the pharynx. (In amphibians respiration takes place by mouth cavity also)

Bud

(1)	In plants, an embryonic shoot, including rudimentary leaves, often protected by special bud scales.

(2)	In animals, an asexually produced outgrowth that develops into a new individual.

Budding

An asexual means of propagation in which outgrowths from the parent form and pinch off to live independently or else remain attached to eventually form extensive colonies.

Buffer

A substance that consists of acid and base forms in solution and that minimizes changes in pH when extraneous acids or bases are added to the solution.

Bulb

A modified bud with thickened leaves adapted for underground food storage.

Bulbils

A small bulb or bulb-shaped growth arising from the leaf axil or in the place of flowers.

Bulbourethral gland

One of a pair of glands near the base of the penis in the human male that secrete a fluid that lubricates and neutralizes acids in the urethra during sexual arousal.

Bulk flow

The movement of water due to a difference in pressure between two locations.

Bundle cap

A bundle cap is a cluster of fibres that covers the top of the top or the phloem side of the vascular bundle.

Bulliform cells

One of the large, highly vacuolated cells occurring in the epidermis of grass leaves. Also known as a motor cell.

Bundle of His

In the vertebrate heart, a group of muscle fibres that carry impulses from the atrioventricular node to the walls of the ventricles; the only electrical bridge between the atria and the ventricles.

C

C_3 pathway

A metabolic pathway where CO_2 is converted to 3-phosphoglycerate, the first stable intermediate organic compound containing three carbon atoms

C_3 plant

A plant that uses the Calvin cycle for the initial steps that incorporate CO_2 into organic material, forming a three-carbon compound as the first stable intermediate.

C_4 pathway

The set of reactions by which some plants initially fix carbon in the four-carbon compound oxaloacetic acid; the carbon dioxide is later released in the interior of the leaf and enters the Calvin cycle.

C$_4$ plant

A plant that prefaces the Calvin cycle with reactions that incorporate CO_2 into four-carbon compounds, the end-product of which supplies CO_2 for the Calvin cycle.

Cartilage

A tough, elastic, fibrous connective tissue found in various parts of the body, such as the joints, outer ear, and larynx. A major constituent of the embryonic and young vertebrate skeleton, it is converted largely to bone with maturation.

Carotenoids

Any of a group of yellow, orange, red, or brown pigments found in many living organisms, particularly in the chloroplasts of plants.

Calcaneum

The quadrangular bone at the back of the tarsus. Also called *heel bone*.

Calcitonin

A mammalian thyroid hormone that lowers blood calcium levels.

Calcium oxalate

A small, colourless crystal that may be present in urine or maybe a component of renal calculi.

Callus

In plants, undifferentiated tissue; a term used in tissue culture, grafting, and wound healing.

Calmodulin

An intracellular protein to which calcium binds in its function as a second messenger in hormone action.

Calorie

The amount of heat energy required to raise the temperature of 1 g of water 1°C; the amount of heat energy that 1 g of water releases when it cools by 1°C. The Calorie (with a capital C), usually used to indicate the energy content of food, is a kilocalorie.

Calvin cycle

The second of two major stages in photosynthesis (following the light reactions), involving atmospheric CO_2 fixation and reduction of the fixed carbon into carbohydrate.

Calyx

Collectively, the sepals of a flower.

CAM photosynthesis

Crassulacean acid metabolism, also known as CAM photosynthesis, is an elaborate carbon fixation pathway in some photosynthetic plants. CAM is usually found in plants living in arid conditions, including cacti and pineapples.

CAM plant

A plant that uses crassulacean acid metabolism, an adaptation for photosynthesis in arid conditions, first discovered in the family Crassulaceae. Carbon dioxide entering open stomata during the night is converted into organic acids, which release CO_2 for the Calvin cycle during the day when stomata are closed.

Cambrian explosion

A burst of evolutionary origins when most of the major body plans of animals appeared in a relatively brief time in geological history; recorded in the fossil record about 545 to 525 million years ago.

Cancer

A serious disease resulting from a malignant growth or tumour, caused by abnormal and uncontrolled cell division.

Canine

One of the four-pointed conical teeth located between the incisors and the premolars.

Canal system

A tube, duct, or passageway.

Capillary

A microscopic blood vessel that penetrates the tissues and consists of a single layer of endothelial cells that allows exchange between the blood and interstitial fluid.

Capillary action

The movement of water or any liquid along a surface; results from the combined effect of cohesion and adhesion.

Capillaries

Capillaries are the smallest of a body's blood vessels.

Capsid

The protein shell that encloses the viral genome; rod-shaped, polyhedral, or more completely shaped.

Capsule

A slimy layer around the cells of certain bacteria.

Copulatory

Coupled; joined

Carapace

A hard bony or chitinous outer covering, such as the fused dorsal plates of a turtle or the portion of the exoskeleton covering the head and thorax of a crustacean.

Carbohydrate

A sugar (monosaccharide) or one of its dimers (disaccharides) or polymers (polysaccharides).

Carbohydrates

Compounds, such as cellulose, sugar, and starch, that contain only carbon, hydrogen, and oxygen, and are a major part of the diets of people and other animals.

Carbon cycle

Worldwide circulation and reutilization of carbon atoms, chiefly due to metabolic processes of living organisms. Inorganic carbon, in the form of carbon dioxide, is incorporated into organic compounds by photosynthetic organisms; when the organic compounds are broken down in respiration, carbon dioxide is released. Large quantities of carbon are "stored" in the seas and the atmosphere, as well as in fossil fuel deposits.

Carbon fixation

The incorporation of carbon from CO_2 into an organic compound by an autotrophic organism (a plant, another photosynthetic organism, or a chemoautotrophic bacterium).

Carbonyl group

A functional group present in aldehydes and ketones, consisting of a carbon atom double-bonded to an oxygen atom.

Carboxyl group

A functional group present in organic acids, consisting of a single carbon atom double-bonded to an oxygen atom and also bonded to a hydroxyl group.

Carcinogen

A chemical agent that causes cancer.

Cardiac muscle

A type of muscle that forms the contractile wall of the heart; its cells are joined by intercalated discs that relay each heartbeat.

Cardiac output

The volume of blood pumped per minute by the left ventricle of the heart.

Cardiac muscle

The specialized striated muscle tissue of the heart; the myocardium.

Cardiovascular system

A closed circulatory system with a heart and branching network of arteries, capillaries, and veins.

Carnivore

An animal, such as a shark, hawk, or spider, that eats other animals.

Carotenoids

Accessory pigments, yellow and orange, in the chloroplasts of plants; by absorbing wavelengths of light that chlorophyll cannot, they broaden the spectrum of colours that can drive photosynthesis.

Carotid arteries

Either of the two principal arteries on both sides of the neck that supply blood to the head and neck. Also known as the common carotid artery.

Carpel

The female reproductive organ of a flower, consisting of the stigma, style, and ovary.

Carrying capacity

The maximum population size that can be supported by the available resources, symbolized as K.

Cartilage

A type of flexible connective tissue with an abundance of collagenous fibres embedded in Chondrin.

Cartilaginous

Having a skeleton consisting mainly of cartilage.

Casparian strip

A water-impermeable ring of wax around endodermal cells in plants that blocks the passive flow of water and solutes into the stele by way of cell walls.

Catabolic pathway

A metabolic pathway that releases energy by breaking down complex molecules into simpler compounds.

Catabolism

Within a cell or organism, the sum of all chemical reactions in which large molecules are broken down into smaller parts.

Catabolite activator protein (CAP)

In E coli, a helper protein that stimulates gene expression by binding within the promoter region of an operon and enhancing the promoter's ability to associate with RNA polymerase.

Catalyst

A substance that lowers the activation energy of a chemical reaction by forming a temporary association with the reacting molecules; as a result, the rate of the reaction is accelerated. Enzymes are catalysts.

Category

In a hierarchical classification system, the level at which a particular group is ranked.

Cation

An ion with a positive charge, produced by the loss of one or more electrons.

Cation exchange

A process in which positively charged minerals are made available to a plant when hydrogen ions in the soil displace mineral ions from the clay particles.

Cdc genes

A gene that regulates the cell cycle. Also known as CDC gene.

Cell

A basic unit of living matter separated from its environment by a plasma membrane; the fundamental structural unit of life.

Cell centre

A region in the cytoplasm near the nucleus from which microtubules originate and radiate.

Cell cycle

An ordered sequence of events in the life of a dividing eukaryotic cell, composed of the M, G_1, S, and G_2 phases.

Cell-cycle control system

A cyclically operating set of proteins that triggers and coordinates events in the eukaryotic cell cycle.

Cell division

The process in reproduction and growth by which a cell divides to form daughter cells.

Cell fractionation

The disruption of a cell and the separation of its organelles by centrifugation.

Cell inclusions

The act of including or the state of being included.

Cell-mediated immunity

The type of immunity that functions in defence against fungi, protists, bacteria, and viruses inside host cells and tissue transplants, with highly specialized cells that circulate in the blood and lymphoid tissue.

Cell membrane

The outer membrane of the cell; the plasma membrane.

Cell organelles

A specialized part of a cell; "the first organelle to be identified as the nucleus".

Cell plate

A double membrane across the midline of a dividing plant cell, between which the new cell wall forms during cytokinesis.

Cell theory

All living things are composed of cells; cells arise only from other cells. No exception has been found to these two principles since they were first proposed well over a century ago.

Cellular

Consisting of or containing a cell or cells

Cellular level

The process that occurs in cellular

Cell wall

A protective layer external to the plasma membrane in plant cells, bacteria, fungi, and some protists. In the case of plant cells, the wall is formed of cellulose fibres embedded in a polysaccharide-protein matrix. The primary cell wall is thin and flexible, whereas the secondary cell wall is stronger and more rigid, and is the primary constituent of wood.

Cellular differentiation

The structural and functional divergence of cells as they become specialized during a multicellular organism's development; dependent on the control of gene expression.

Cellular respiration

The most prevalent and efficient catabolic pathway for the production of ATP, in which oxygen is consumed as a reactant along with the organic fuel.

Cellulose

A structural polysaccharide of cell walls, consisting of glucose monomers joined by (1-4) glycosidic linkages.

Celsius scale

A temperature scale (°C) equal to 5/9 (°F – 32) that measures the freezing point of water at 0°C and the boiling point of water at 100°C.

Centrifugation process

An apparatus in which humans or animals are enclosed and which is revolved to simulate the effects of acceleration in a spacecraft.

Centipede

A small wormlike creature with many legs.

Centrioles

One of two cylindrical cellular structures that are composed of nine triplet microtubules and form the asters during mitosis.

The central nervous system (CNS)

In vertebrate animals, the brain and spinal cord.

Centrifugation

Centrifugation is a process that involves the use of the centrifugal force for the separation of mixtures.

Centriole

A structure in an animal cell, composed of cylinders of microtubule triplets arranged in a 9 + 0 pattern. An animal cell usually has a pair of centrioles, which are involved in cell division.

Centromere

The centralized region joining two sister chromatids.

Centrosome

The material present in the cytoplasm of all eukaryotic cells and important during cell division; also called the microtubule-organizing centre.

Cephalochordate

A chordate without a backbone, represented by lancelets, tiny marine animals.

Cerebellum

Part of the vertebrate hindbrain (rhombencephalon) located dorsally; functions in unconscious coordination of movement and balance.

Cerebral cortex

The surface of the cerebrum; the largest and most complex part of the mammalian brain, containing sensory and motor nerve cell bodies of the cerebrum; the part of the vertebrate brain most changed through evolution.

Cerebral ganglia

They transmit nerve pulse activity so nerve cells can 'talk' to each other.

Cerebral hemispheres

Either of the two symmetrical halves of the cerebrum, as divided by the longitudinal cerebral fissure.

Cerebroside

Any of various lipid compounds containing glucose or galactose and glucose, and found in the brain and other nerve tissue.

Cerebrum

The dorsal portion, composed of the right and left hemispheres, of the vertebrate forebrain; the integrating centre for memory, learning, emotions, and other highly complex functions of the central nervous system.

Chaparral

A scrubland biome of dense, spiny evergreen shrubs found at midlatitudes along coasts where cold ocean currents circulate offshore; characterized by mild, rainy winters and long, hot, dry summers.

Character displacement

A phenomenon in which species that live together in the same environment tend to diverge in those characteristics that overlap; exemplified by Darwin's finches.

Chelonia

An order of the Reptilia, subclass Anapsida, including the turtles, terrapins, and tortoises.

Chemical bond

An attraction between two atoms resulting from a sharing of outer-shell electrons or the presence of opposite charges on the atoms; the bonded atoms gain complete outer electron shells.

Chemical equilibrium

In a reversible chemical reaction, the point at which the rate of the forward reaction equals the rate of the reverse reaction.

Chemical reaction

A process leading to chemical changes in the matter; involves the making and/or breaking of chemical bonds.

Chemiosmosis

The production of ATP using the energy of hydrogen-ion gradients across membranes to phosphorylate ADP; powers most ATP synthesis in cells.

Chemiosmotic coupling

The mechanism by which ADP is phosphorylated to ATP in mitochondria and chloroplasts. The energy released as electrons pass down an electron transport chain is used to establish a proton gradient across an inner membrane of the organelle; when protons subsequently flow down this electrochemical gradient, the potential energy released is captured in the terminal phosphate bonds of ATP.

Chemoautotroph

An organism that needs only carbon dioxide as a carbon source but that obtains energy by oxidizing inorganic substances.

Chemoheterotroph

An organism that must consume organic molecules for both energy and carbon.

Chemoreceptor

A receptor that transmits information about the total solute concentration in a solution or about individual kinds of molecules.

Chemosynthetic

Applied to autotrophic bacteria that use the energy released by specific inorganic reactions to power their life processes, including the synthesis of organic molecules.

Chewing

The movements of the mandible during mastication; controlled by neuromuscular action and limited by the anatomic structure of the temporomandibular joints.

Chiasma

The X-shaped, microscopically visible region representing homologous chromatids that have exchanged genetic material through crossing over during meiosis.

Chitin

A structural polysaccharide of an amino sugar found in many fungi and the exoskeletons of all arthropods.

Chitinous

A tough, protective, semitransparent substance, primarily a nitrogen-containing polysaccharide, forming the principal component of arthropod exoskeletons and the cell walls of certain fungi.

Choanocyte

Any of the flagellated cells in sponges having a collar of cytoplasm around the flagellum; they maintain a flow of water through the body.

Chlorophylls

A green pigment located within the chloroplasts of plants; chlorophyll-a can participate directly in the light reactions, which convert solar energy to chemical energy.

Chloroplast

An organelle found only in plants and photosynthetic protists that absorbs sunlight and uses it to drive the synthesis of organic compounds from carbon dioxide and water.

Cholesterol

The steroid that forms an essential component of animal cell membranes and acts as a precursor molecule for the synthesis of other biologically important steroids.

Chondrichthyes

The vertebrate class of cartilaginous fishes, represented by sharks and their relatives.

Chondrin

A protein-carbohydrate complex secreted by chondrocytes; chondrin and collagen fibres form cartilage.

Chordate

A member of a diverse phylum of animals that possess a notochord; a dorsal, hollow nerve cord; pharyngeal gill slits; and a postanal tail as embryos.

Chorion

The outermost of four extraembryonic membranes; contributes to the formation of the mammalian placenta.

Chorionic villus sampling (CVS)

A technique for diagnosing genetic and congenital defects while the fetus is in the uterus. A small sample of the fetal portion of the placenta is removed and analyzed.

Chromatid

Either of the two strands of a replicated chromosome, which are joined at the centromere.

Chromatin

The complex of DNA and proteins that makes up a eukaryotic chromosome. When the cell is not dividing, chromatin exists as a mass of very long, thin fibres that are not visible with a light microscope.

Chromista

In some classification systems, a kingdom consisting of brown algae, golden algae, and diatoms.

Chromoplasts

A plastid contains pigments other than chlorophyll, usually yellow or orange carotenoids.

Chromosomes

A threadlike, gene-carrying structure found in the nucleus. Each chromosome consists of one very long DNA molecule and associated proteins.

Chromosome map

A diagram of the linear order of the genes on a chromosome.

Chromatophores

A pigment-containing or pigment-producing cell, especially in certain lizards, that by expansion or contraction can change the colour of the skin. Also called *pigment cell*.

Chytrid

A fungus with flagellated stage; the possible evolutionary link between fungi and protists.

Cilium

A short cellular appendage specialized for locomotion, formed from a core of nine outer doublet microtubules and two inner single microtubules ensheathed in an extension of the plasma membrane.

Circadian rhythms

A physiological cycle of about 24 hours, present in all eukaryotic organisms, that persists even in the absence of external cues.

Circulation

The flow of blood from the heart through the arteries, and then back through the veins to the heart, where the cycle is renewed.

Circulatory

Relating to blood circulation or the circulatory system.

Cirrus

A slender flexible appendage, such as the fused cilia of certain protozoans.

Cladistics

A taxonomic approach that classifies organisms according to the order in time at which branches arise along a phylogenetic tree, without considering the degree of morphological divergence.

Cladogenesis

A pattern of evolutionary change that produces biological diversity by budding one or more new species from a parent species that continues to exist; also called branching evolution.

Cladogram

A dichotomous phylogenetic tree that branches repeatedly, suggesting a classification of organisms based on the time sequence in which evolutionary branches arise.

Cladophylls

A photosynthetic branch or portion of a stem that resembles and functions as a leaf, as in the asparagus. Also called cladode.

Clasper

Any of the appendages of the male of certain insects and crustaceans that are used during copulation to hold the female.

Class

A taxonomic grouping of related, similar orders; category above order and below phylum.

Classical conditioning

A type of associative learning; the association of a normally irrelevant stimulus with a fixed behavioural response.

Classification

The systematic grouping of organisms into categories based on evolutionary or structural relationships between them., A division or category in a classifying system.

Cleavage

The process of cytokinesis in animal cells, characterized by pinching of the plasma membrane; specifically, the succession of rapid cell divisions without growth during early embryonic development that converts the zygote into a ball of cells.

Cleavage furrow

The first sign of cleavage in an animal cell; a shallow groove in the cell surface near the old metaphase plate.

Cline

Variation in features of individuals in a population that parallels a gradient in the environment.

Clitoris

A small elongated erectile organ at the anterior part of the vulva, homologous with the penis, present in female

Cloaca

A common opening for the digestive, urinary, and reproductive tracts in all vertebrates except most mammals.

Clonal selection

The mechanism that determines the specificity and accounts for antigen memory in the immune system; occurs because an antigen introduced into the body selectively activates only a tiny fraction of inactive lymphocytes, which proliferate to form a clone of effector cells specific for the stimulating antigen.

Clone

(1)   A lineage of genetically identical individuals or cells.

(2)   In popular usage, a single individual organism that is genetically identical to another individual.

Cloning vector

An agent used to transfer DNA in genetic engineerings, such as a plasmid that moves recombinant DNA from a test tube back into a cell, or a virus that transfers recombinant DNA by infection.

Closed circulatory system

A type of internal transport in which blood is confined to vessels.

Cnidaria

Phylum Cnidaria includes animals like hydras; polyps; jellyfishes; sea anemones; corals

Cnidocyte

A stinging cell containing a nematocyst; characteristic of cnidarians.

Cnidarians

Cnidarians are the group of invertebrate animals which possess stinging cells called cnidocytes

Cnidoblast

A cell in the epidermis of coelenterates in which a nematocyst is developed.

Cocci

Any spherical or nearly spherical bacteria

Cochlea

The complex, coiled organ of hearing that contains the organ of Corti.

Codominance

A phenotypic situation in which both alleles are expressed in the heterozygote.

Codon

A three-nucleotide sequence of DNA or mRNA that specifies a particular amino acid or termination signal; the basic unit of the genetic code.

Coelom

A body cavity completely lined with mesoderm.

Coelomate

An animal whose body cavity is completely lined by mesoderm, the layers of which connect dorsally and ventrally to form mesenteries.

Coenocytic

Referring to a multinucleated condition resulting from the repeated division of nuclei without cytoplasmic division.

Coenzyme

An organic molecule serving as a cofactor. Most vitamins function as coenzymes in important metabolic reactions.

Coevolution

The mutual influence on the evolution of two different species interacting with each other and reciprocally influencing each other's adaptations.

Cofactor

Any nonprotein molecule or ion that is required for the proper functioning of an enzyme. Cofactors can be permanently bound to the active site or may bind loosely with the substrate during catalysis.

Cohesion

The binding together of like molecules, often by hydrogen bonds.

Cohesion species concept

The idea that specific evolutionary adaptations and discrete complexes of genes define species.

Cohesion-tension theory

A theory accounting for the upward movement of water in plants. According to this theory, transpiration of a water molecule results in a negative (below 1 atmosphere) pressure in the leaf cells, inducing the entrance from the vascular tissue of another water molecule, which, because of the cohesive property of water, pulls with it a chain of water molecules extending up from the cells of the root tip.

Cold acclimation response

The process by which plants increase their tolerance to freezing by exposure to low, nonfreezing temperatures.

Coleoptile

The sheath enclosing the apical meristem and leaf primordia of a germinating monocot.

Coleorhizae

A protective sheath enclosing the embryonic root of grasses.

Collagen

A glycoprotein in the extracellular matrix of animal cells that forms strong fibres found extensively in connective tissue and bone; the most abundant protein in the animal kingdom.

Collecting duct

The location in the kidney where filtrate from renal tubules is collected; the filtrate is now called urine.

Collenchyma cell

A flexible plant cell type that occurs in strands or cylinders that support young parts of the plant without restraining growth.

Cholesterol metabolism

A white crystalline substance, $C_{27}H_{45}OH$, found in animal tissues and various foods, that is normally synthesized by the liver and is important as a constituent of cell membranes and a precursor to steroid hormones. Its level in the bloodstream can influence the pathogenesis of certain conditions, such as the development of atherosclerotic plaque and coronary artery disease.

Colonial

Living in, consisting of, or forming a colony. An inhabitant of a colony.

Colony

A group of organisms of the same species living together in close association.

Columnar

In biology, columnar refers to the shape of epithelial cells that are taller than they are wide

Commensalism

A symbiotic relationship in which the symbiont benefits but the host is neither helped nor harmed.

Community

All the organisms that inhabit a particular area; an assemblage of populations of different species living close enough together for potential interaction.

Companion cell

A type of plant cell that is connected to a sieve-tube member by many plasmodesmata and whose nucleus and ribosomes may serve one or more adjacent, sieve-tube members.

Competition

Interaction between members of the same population or two or more populations using the same resource, often present in limited supply.

Competitive exclusion principle

The concept that when the populations of two species compete for the same limited resources, one population will use the resources more efficiently and have a reproductive advantage that will eventually lead to the elimination of the other population.

Competitive inhibitor

A substance that reduces the activity of an enzyme by entering the active site in place of the substrate whose structure it mimics.

Complement fixation

An immune response in which antigen-antibody complexes activate complement proteins.

Complement system

A group of at least 20 blood proteins that cooperate with other defence mechanisms; may amplify the inflammatory response, enhance phagocytosis, or directly lyse pathogens; activated by the onset of the immune response or by surface antigens on microorganisms or other foreign cells.

Complementary DNA (cDNA)

A DNA molecule made in vitro using mRNA as a template and the enzyme reverse transcriptase. A cDNA molecule, therefore, corresponds to a gene but lacks the introns present in the DNA of the genome.

Complete digestive tract

A digestive tube that runs between a mouth and an anus; also called an alimentary canal. An incomplete digestive tract has only one opening.

Complete flower

A flower that has sepals, petals, stamens, and carpels.

Complex tissues

The complex tissues include the dermal and vascular tissues of plants.

Compound

A chemical combination, in a fixed ratio, of two or more elements.

Compound eye

A type of multifaceted eye in insects and crustaceans consisting of up to several thousand light-detecting, focusing ommatidia; especially good at detecting movement.

Compound leaf

a leaf that is composed of two or more leaflets on a common stalk. Clover, roses, sumac, and walnut trees have compound leaves.

Concentric

Having a common centre.

Concentration gradient

A regular increase or decrease in the intensity or density of a chemical substance. Cells often maintain concentration gradients of H^+ ions across their membranes. When a gradient exists, the ions or other chemical substances involved tend to move from where they are more concentrated to where they are less concentrated.

Condensation

The process of changing from a gaseous to a liquid or solid-state.

Condensation reaction

A reaction in which two molecules become covalently bonded to each other through the loss of a small molecule, usually water; also called a dehydration reaction.

Condyle

A round bump on a bone where it forms a joint with another bone.

Cone cell

(1)   In plants, the reproductive structure of a conifer.

(2)   In vertebrates, a type of photoreceptor cell in the retina, concerned with the perception of colour and with the most acute discrimination of detail.

Conical

Relating to or resembling a cone

Conidium

A naked, asexual spore produced at the ends of hyphae in ascomycetes.

Conifer

A gymnosperm whose reproductive structure is the cone. Conifers include pines, firs, redwoods, and other large trees.

Conjoint

Xylem and phloem are together in the same vascular *bundle*.

Conjoint bundles

Conjoint vascular bundles xylem and phloem occurs in the same vascular bundle on the same radius that is one above the other

Conjugation

In bacteria, the transfer of DNA between two cells that are temporarily joined.

Connective tissues

Animal tissue that functions mainly to bind and support other tissues, having a sparse population of cells scattered through an extracellular matrix.

Conservation biology

A goal-oriented science that seeks to counter the biodiversity crisis, the current rapid decrease in Earth's variety of life.

Consumer, in ecological systems

A heterotroph that derives its energy from living or freshly killed organisms or parts thereof. Primary consumers are herbivores; higher-level consumers are carnivores.

Continental drift

The gradual movement of the Earth's continents that has occurred over hundreds of millions of years.

Continuous fibres

A material consisting of extremely fine glass fibres, used in making various products, such as yarns, fabrics, insulators, and structural objects or parts. Also called *spun glass*.

Continuous variation

A gradation of small differences in a particular trait, such as height, within a population; occurs in traits that are controlled by many genes.

Contraception

The prevention of pregnancy.

Contractile roots

Contractile roots are found in many plants species mainly at the base of an underground organ (bulb, corm, succulent rosette, etc.).

Contractile vacuoles

A small fluid-filled cavity in the cytoplasm of certain unicellular organisms; it gradually increases in size and then collapses; its function is thought to be respiratory and excretory.

Conus arteriosus

The cone-shaped projection from which the pulmonary artery arises on the right ventricle of the heart in man and mammals.

Convection

The mass movement of warmed air or liquid to or from the surface of a body or object.

Convergent evolution

The independent development of similarity between species as a result of their having similar ecological roles and selection pressures.

Cooperativity

Interaction of the constituent subunits of a protein causing a conformational change in one subunit to be transmitted to all the others.

Copulation

The sexual union of two individuals, resulting in insemination or deposition of the male gametes in proximity to the female gametes.

Cork

A secondary tissue that is a major constituent of bark in woody and some herbaceous plants; made up of flattened cells, dead at maturity; restricts gas and water exchange and protects the vascular tissues from injury.

Cork cambium

A cylinder of meristematic tissue in plants that produces cork cells to replace the epidermis during secondary growth.

Corolla

Petals, collectively; usually the conspicuously coloured flower parts.

Corpuscle

Any of various cellular or small multicellular structures in the body, especially a red or white blood cell.

Corpus callosum

In the vertebrate brain, a tightly packed mass of myelinated nerve fibres connecting the two cerebral hemispheres.

Corpus lutuem

A secreting tissue in the ovary that forms from the collapsed follicle after ovulation and produces progesterone.

Corpuscles

A rounded globular mass of cells, such as the pressure receptor on certain nerve endings.

Cortex

(1) The outer, as opposed to the inner, part of an organ, as in the adrenal gland. (2) In a stem or root, the primary tissue bounded externally by the epidermis and internally by the central cylinder of vascular tissue.

Cortisol

A steroid hormone, produced by the adrenal cortex, that promotes the formation of glucose from protein and fat; also suppresses the inflammatory and immune responses.

Cotransport

The coupling of the "downhill" diffusion of one substance to the "uphill" transport of another against its concentration gradient.

Cotyledon

The one (monocot) or two (dicot) seed leaves of an angiosperm embryo.

Countercurrent exchange

The opposite flow of adjacent fluids that maximizes transfer rates; for example, blood in the gills flows in the opposite direction in which water passes over the gills, maximizing oxygen uptake and carbon dioxide loss.

Coupled reactions

In cells, the linking of endergonic (energy-requiring) reactions to exergonic (energy- releasing) reactions that provide enough energy to drive the endergonic reactions forward.

Covalent bond

A chemical bond formed as a result of the sharing of one or more pairs of electrons.

Crassulacean acid metabolism

A process by which some species of plants in hot, dry climates take in carbon dioxide during the night, fixing it in organic acids; the carbon dioxide is released during the day and used immediately in the Calvin cycle.

Cranial

Relating to the skull or cranium.

Cretaceous

Belonging to the geologic time, system of rocks, and sedimentary deposits of the third and last period of the Mesozoic Era, characterized by the development of flowering plants and ending with the sudden extinction of the dinosaurs and many other forms of life.

Crista

An infolding of the inner membrane of a mitochondrion that houses the electron transport chain and the enzyme catalyzing the synthesis of ATP.

Crop

Cultivated plants or agricultural produce, such as grain, vegetables, or fruit, considered as a group: *Wheat is a common crop.*

Cross-fertilization

The fusion of gametes formed by different individuals; as opposed to self-fertilization.

Crossing over

The reciprocal exchange of genetic material between non-sister chromatids during synapsis of meiosis I.

Cryptic colouration

A type of camouflage that makes potential prey difficult to spot against its background.

Ctenidia

A comblike respiratory structure serving as the gill of certain molluscs.

Ctenoid

Having marginal projections that resemble the teeth of a comb: *a ctenoid fish.*

Cuboidal ciliated epithelium

Cuboidal epithelia are epithelial cells having a cube-like shape; that is, their width is approximately equal to their height. They may exist in single layers (simple cuboidal epithelium) or multiple layers (stratified cuboidal epithelium) depending on their location (and thus function) in the body.

Cutaneous

Relating to the skin or Integumentary system (skin).

Cuticle

(1)   A waxy covering on the surface of stems and leaves that acts as an adaptation to prevent desiccation in terrestrial plants.

(2)   The exoskeleton of an arthropod, consisting of layers of protein and chitin that are variously modified for different functions.

Cutin

A waxlike, water-repellent material present in the walls of some plant cells and forming the cuticle, which covers the epidermis.

Cyanobacteria

Photosynthetic, oxygen-producing bacteria (formerly known as blue-green algae).

Cyclic AMP

Cyclic adenosine monophosphate, a ring-shaped molecule made from ATP that is a common intracellular signalling molecule (second messenger) in eukaryotic cells, for example, in vertebrate endocrine cells. It is also a regulator of some bacterial operons.

Cyclic electron flow

A route of electron flow during the light reactions of photosynthesis that involves the only photosystem I and produces ATP but not NADPH or oxygen.

Cyclin

A regulatory protein whose concentration fluctuates cyclically.

Cyclin-dependent kinase (Cdk)

A protein kinase that is active only when attached to a particular cyclin.

Cycloid

Thin, rounded, and smooth-edged; disklike. Used of fish scales.

Cyclosis or rotation

The circulation of cytoplasm within a cell is called a cyclosis or rotation.

Cyclostomata

A subclass comprising the simplest and most primitive of living vertebrates characterized by the absence of jaws and the presence of a single median nostril and an uncalcified cartilaginous skeleton.

Cymose

Having a usually flat-topped flower cluster in which the main and branch stems each end in a flower that opens before those below it or to its side.

Cystolith

Cystolith is a botanical term for the inorganic concretions, usually of calcium carbonate, formed in a cellulose matrix in special cells, generally in the leaf of plants of certain families.

E.g. *ficus elastic,* the Indian rubber plant.

Cytochrome

An iron-containing protein, a component of electron transport chains in mitochondria and chloroplasts.

Cytokines

In the vertebrate immune system, protein factors secreted by macrophages and helper T cells as regulators of neighbouring cells.

Cytokinesis

The division of the cytoplasm to form two separate daughter cells immediately after mitosis.

Cytokinin

A class of related plant hormones that retard ageing and act in concert with auxins to stimulate cell division, influence the pathway of differentiation, and control apical dominance.

Cytoplasm

The entire contents of the cell, exclusive of the nucleus, and bounded by the plasma membrane.

Cytoplasmic determinants

In animal development, substances deposited by the mother in the eggs she produces that regulate the expression of genes affecting the early development of the embryo.

Cytoplasmic streaming

A circular flow of cytoplasm, involving myosin and actin filaments, that speeds the distribution of materials within cells.

Cytoskeleton

A network of microtubules, microfilaments, and intermediate filaments that branch throughout the cytoplasm and serve a variety of mechanical and transport functions. **Cytosol**

The semifluid portion of the cytoplasm.

Cytotoxic T cell (TC)

A type of lymphocyte that kills infected cells and cancer cells.

Concentric rings

Having a common centre " concentric rings"

D

Dalton

The atomic mass unit; a measure of mass for atoms and subatomic particles.

Darwinian fitness

A measure of the relative contribution of an individual to the gene pool of the next generation.

Daughter cell

A cell that is the offspring of a cell that has undergone mitosis or meiosis. The term "daughter" does not indicate the sex of the cell.

Day-neutral plant

A plant whose flowering is not affected by photoperiod.

Deciduous

Refers to plants that shed their leaves at a certain season.

Decomposers

Saprotrophic fungi and bacteria that absorb nutrients from nonliving organic material such as corpses, fallen plant material, and the wastes of living organisms, and convert them into inorganic forms.

Dehydration reaction

A chemical reaction in which two molecules covalently bond to one another with the removal of a water molecule.

Deletion

A deficiency in a chromosome resulting from the loss of a fragment through breakage

Demography

The study of statistics relating to births and deaths in populations.

Denaturation

For proteins, a process in which a protein unravels and loses its native conformation, thereby becoming biologically inactive. For DNA, the separation of the two strands of the double helix. Denaturation occurs under extreme conditions of pH, salt concentration, and temperature.

Dendrite

One of the usually numerous, short, highly branched processes of a neuron that conveys nerve impulses toward the cell body.

Denitrification

The process by which certain bacteria living in poorly aerated soils break down nitrates,   using the oxygen for their respiration and releasing nitrogen back into the atmosphere.

Density

The number of individuals per unit area or volume.

Density-dependent factor

Any factor influencing population regulation that has a greater impact as population density increases.

Density-dependent inhibition

The phenomenon observed in normal animal cells that causes them to stop dividing when they come into contact with one another.

Density-independent factors

Any factor influencing population regulation that acts to reduce the population by the same percentage, regardless of size.

Deoxyribonucleic acid (DNA)

A double-stranded, helical nucleic acid molecule capable of replicating and determining the inherited structure of a cell's proteins.

Deoxyribose

The sugar component of DNA, having one less hydroxyl group than ribose, the sugar component of RNA.

Dependent variable

In an experiment, the dependent variable is the factor that responds when another factor is manipulated.

Deploblastic

Derived from two embryonic germs layers, the ectoderm and endoderm. Used of lower invertebrates, such as sponges and coelenterates.

Depolarization

An electrical state in an excitable cell whereby the inside of the cell is made less negative relative to the outside than at the resting membrane potential. A neuron membrane is depolarized if a stimulus decreases its voltage from the resting potential of -70 mV in the direction of zero voltage.

Deposit-feeder

A heterotroph, such as an earthworm, that eats its way through detritus, salvaging bits and pieces of decaying organic matter.

Dermal tissue system

The protective covering of plants; generally a single layer of tightly packed epidermal cells covering young plant organs formed by primary growth.

Dermis

The inner layer of the skin, beneath the epidermis.

Desmosome

A type of intercellular junction in animal cells that functions as an anchor.

Determinate cleavage

A type of embryonic development in protostomes that rigidly casts the developmental fate of each embryonic cell very early.

Determinate growth

A type of growth characteristic of animals, in which the organism stops growing after it reaches a certain size.

Determination

The progressive restriction of developmental potential, causing the possible fate of each cell to become more limited as the embryo develops.

Detritus

Dead organic matter.

Detritivores

Organisms that live on dead and discarded organic matter; include large scavengers, smaller animals such as earthworms and some insects, as well as decomposers (fungi and bacteria).

Deuterostome

One of two distinct evolutionary lines of coelomates, consisting of the echinoderms and chordates and characterized by radial, indeterminate cleavage, enterococcus formation of the coelom, and development of the anus from the blastopore.

Development

The progressive production of the phenotypic characteristics of a multicellular organism, beginning with the fertilization of an egg.

Diadelphous

Having the filaments of a flower united into two groups

Diakinesis

In cell division, the stage of first meiotic prophase, in which the nucleolus and nuclear envelope disappear and the spindle fibres form.

Diaphragm

A sheet of muscle that forms the bottom wall of the thoracic cavity in mammals; active in ventilating the lungs.

Diastole

The stage of the heart cycle in which the heart muscle is relaxed, allowing the chambers to fill with blood.

Diatoms

Any of numerous microscopic, unicellular, marine or freshwater algae of the phylum Chrysophyta, having cell walls containing silica.

Diastolic pressure

The pressure in an artery during the ventricular relaxation phase of the heart cycle.

Dichlamydeous

Having two coverings, a calyx and a corolla.

Dicot

A subdivision of flowering plants whose members possess two embryonic seed leaves, or cotyledons.

Dicotyledon

A member of the class of flowering plants having two seed leaves, or cotyledons, among other distinguishing features; often abbreviated as a dicot.

Dictyosomes

The Golgi apparatus in plant cells.

Differentiation

The process by which cells or tissues change a more specialized form or function, especially during embryonic development.

Diffusion

The spontaneous tendency of a substance to move down its concentration gradient from a more concentrated to a less concentrated area.

Digestion

The process of breaking down food into molecules small enough for the body to absorb.

Digestive tract

The series of organs in the digestive system through which food passes, nutrients are absorbed, and waste is eliminated. In higher vertebrates, it consists of the oesophagus, stomach, small and large intestines, rectum, and anus.

Dihybrid

A hybrid individual that is heterozygous for two genes or two characters.

Dihybrid cross

A breeding experiment in which parental varieties differing in two traits is mated.

Dikaryon

A mycelium of certain septate fungi that possesses two separate haploid nuclei per cell.

Dioecious

Referring to a plant species that has staminate and carpellate flowers on separate plants.

Dimorphism

Displaying two separate growth forms.

Dipeptides

A dipeptide is a molecule consisting of two amino acids joined by a single peptide bond.

Diploid cell

A cell containing two sets of chromosomes (2n), one set inherited from each parent.

Diplomatic

They have two germ layers - or a two-layered body wall. The epidermis and gastrodermis.

Diplotene

A stage of meiotic prophase in which homologous chromosome pairs begin to separate and chiasmata become visible.

Directed molecular evolution

A laboratory version of evolution at the molecular level that can produce "designer molecules." A large starting population of molecules (typically nucleic acids) that varies randomly in base sequence and shape is subjected to replication with variation, followed by selection. After several cycles of replication and selection, the population of molecules will evolve toward one containing a high proportion of molecules well adapted to the selection criterion applied.

Directional selection

The natural selection that favours individuals on one end of the phenotypic range.

Disaccharide

A double sugar, consisting of two monosaccharides joined by dehydration synthesis.

Diurnal

Applied to organisms that are active during the daylight hours.

Dispersion

The distribution of individuals within geographical population boundaries.

Diversifying selection

The natural selection that favours extreme over intermediate phenotypes.

Division

A taxonomic grouping of related, similar classes; a high- level category below kingdom and above class. The division is generally used in the classification of prokaryotes, algae, fungi, and plants, whereas an equivalent category, phylum, is used in the classification of protozoa and animals.

DNA

Abbreviation of deoxyribonucleic acid.

DNA ligase

width="400" valign="TOP"> A linking enzyme essential for DNA replication; catalyzes the covalent bonding of the 3' end of a new DNA fragment to the 5' end of a growing chain.

DNA methylation

The addition of methyl groups ($-CH_3$) to bases of DNA after DNA synthesis; may serve as the long-term control of gene expression.

DNA molecules

A nucleic acid that carries the genetic information in the cell and is capable of self-replication and synthesis of RNA. DNA consists of two long chains of nucleotides twisted into a double helix and joined by hydrogen bonds between the complementary bases adenine and thymine or cytosine and guanine. The sequence of nucleotides determines individual hereditary characteristics.

DNA polymerase

An enzyme that catalyzes the elongation of new DNA at a replication fork by the addition of nucleotides to the existing chain.

DNA probe

A chemically synthesized, radioactively labelled segment of nucleic acid used to find a gene of interest by hydrogen-bonding to a complementary sequence.

Domain

A taxonomic category above the kingdom level; the three domains are Archaea, Bacteria, and Eukarya.

Dominance hierarchy

A linear "pecking order" of animals, where position dictates characteristic social behaviours.

Dominant allele

In a heterozygote, the allele that is fully expressed in the phenotype.

Dormancy

A period during which growth ceases and metabolic activity is greatly reduced; dormancy is broken when certain requirements, for example, of temperature, moisture, or day length, are met.

Dorsal

About or situated near the back; opposite of ventral.

Dorsoventrally

Relating to or involving, or extending along the axis joining the dorsal and ventral sides.

Double circulation

A circulation scheme with separate pulmonary and systemic circuits, which ensures vigorous blood flow to all organs.

Double fertilization

A mechanism of fertilization in angiosperms, in which two sperm cells unite with two cells in the embryo sac to form the zygote and endosperm.

Doublehelix

The form of native DNA, referring to its two adjacent polynucleotide strands wound into a spiral shape.

Down syndrome

A human genetic disease resulting from having an extra chromosome 21, characterized by mental retardation and heart and respiratory defects.

Dorsifixed

Attached at the or by the back to a plant or plant part.

Duodenum

The first section of the small intestine, where acid chyme from the stomach mixes with digestive juices from the pancreas, liver, gallbladder, and gland cells of the intestinal wall.

Duplication

An aberration in chromosome structure resulting from an error in meiosis or mutagens; duplication of a portion of a chromosome resulting from fusion with a fragment from a homologous chromosome.

Duramen (Heartwood)

The older inactive central wood of a tree or woody plant; usually darker and denser than the surrounding sapwood

Dynein

A large contractile protein forming the sidearms of microtubule doublets in cilia and flagella.

E

Ebracteate

Having no bracts.

Ecdysis

The shedding of an outer integument or layer of skin, as by insects, crustaceans, and snakes; moulting.

Ecdysone

A steroid hormone that triggers moulting in arthropods.

Ecological efficiency

The ratio of net productivity at one trophic level to net productivity at the next lower level.

Ecological niche

The total of an organism's utilization of the biotic and abiotic resources of its environment.

Ecological pyramid

A graphic representation of the quantitative relationships of numbers of organisms, biomass, or energy flow between the trophic levels of an ecosystem. Because large amounts of energy and biomass are dissipated at every trophic level, these diagrams nearly always take the form of pyramids.

Ecological species concept

The idea that ecological roles (niches) define species.

Ecological succession

Transition in the species composition of a biological community, often following ecological disturbance of the community; the establishment of a biological community in an area virtually barren of life.

Ecology

The study of how organisms interact with their environments.

Ecosystem

A level of ecological study that includes all the organisms in a given area as well as the abiotic factors with which they interact; a community and its physical environment.

Ecotype

A locally adapted variant of a species, differing genetically from other ecotypes of the same species.

Ectoderm

The outermost of the three primary germ layers in animal embryos; gives rise to the outer covering and, in some phyla, the nervous system, inner ear, and lens of the eye.

Ectoparasites

A parasite, such as a flea, that lives on the exterior of another organism.

Ectotherm

An animal such as a reptile, fish, or amphibian, that must use environmental energy and behavioural adaptations to regulate its body temperature.

Effector cell

A lymphocyte (as a T cell) that has been induced to differentiate into a form (as a cytotoxic T cell) capable of mounting aspecific immune response called also *effector lymphocyte.*

Ectothermic

Relating to an organism that regulates its body temperature largely by exchanging heat with its surrounding environment.

Efferent

Carrying away from a centre, applied to nerves and blood vessels.

Egg

A female gamete, which usually contains abundant cytoplasm and yolk; nonmotile and often larger than a male gamete.

Ejaculatory duct

In the male, a duct from each testis that joins to form the urethra.

Elasmobranches

Any of numerous fishes of the class Chondrichthyes characterized by a cartilaginous skeleton and placoid scales: sharks; rays; skates

Elastin

Elastin is a protein in connective tissue that is elastic and allows many tissues in the body to resume their shape after stretching or contracting. Elastin helps skin to return to its original when it is poked or pinched.

Electric potential

The difference in the amount of electric charge between a region of positive charge and a region of negative charge. The establishment of electric potentials across the plasma membrane and organelle membranes makes possible several phenomena, including the chemiosmotic synthesis of ATP, the conduction of nerve impulses, and muscle contraction.

Electrochemical gradient

The diffusion gradient of an ion, representing a type of potential energy that accounts for both the concentration difference of the ion across a membrane and its tendency to move relative to the membrane potential.

Electrogenic pump

An ion transport protein generating a voltage across the membrane.

Electromagnetic spectrum

The entire spectrum of radiation; ranges in wavelength from less than a nanometer to more than a kilometre.

Electron

A particle with a single negative charge; one or more electrons orbit the nucleus of the atom.

Electron acceptor

A substance that accepts or receives electrons in an oxidation-reduction reaction, becoming reduced in the process.

Electron carrier

A molecule that conveys electrons; one of several membrane proteins in electron transport chains in cells. Electron carriers shuttle electrons during the redox reactions that release energy used to make ATP.

Electron donor

A substance that donates or gives up electrons in an oxidation-reduction reaction, becoming oxidized in the process.

Electron microscope (EM)

A microscope that focuses an electron beam through a specimen, resulting in resolving power a thousandfold greater than that of a light microscope. A transmission electron microscope (TEM) is used to study the internal structure of thin sections of cells. A scanning electron microscope (SEM) is used to study the fine details of cell surfaces.

Electron microscopic

Of or relating to or involving an electron microscope.

Electron shell

An energy level at which an electron orbits the nucleus of an atom.

Electron transport chain

A sequence of electron-carrier molecules (membrane proteins) that shuttle electrons during the redox reactions that release energy used to make ATP.

Electronegativity

The tendency for an atom to pull electrons toward itself.

Element

Any substance that cannot be broken down to any other substance.

Embryo

A developing stage of multicellular organisms; in humans, the stage in the development of offspring from the first division of the zygote until body structures begin to appear; about the ninth week of gestation.

Embryoblast

A group of cells near the embryonic axis of the blastocyst that develops into the embryo.

Embryogenesis

The development and growth of an embryo.

Embryonic germ-layers

The primary germ layers (endoderm, mesoderm, and ectoderm) are formed and organized in their proper locations during gastrulation.

Embryo sac

The female gametophyte of angiosperms, formed from the growth and division of the megaspore into a multicellular structure with eight haploid nuclei.

Enantiomer

One of a pair of molecules that are mirror-image isomers of each other.

Encystment

The process of forming or becoming enclosed in a cyst or capsule.

Endarch xylem

A primary xylem strand in which the first-formed elements are

closest to the centre of the axis, as in the shoots of most Spermatophyta.

Endangered species

A species that is in danger of extinction throughout all or a significant portion of its range.

Endemic species

Species that are confined to a specific, relatively small geographic area.

Endemic

An organism found only in one particular location.

Endergonic reaction

A nonspontaneous chemical reaction in which free energy is absorbed from the surroundings.

Endocarp

The hard inner (usually woody) layer of the pericarp of some fruits (as peaches or plums or cherries or olives) that contains the seed

Endocrine gland

A ductless gland that secretes hormones directly into the bloodstream.

Endocrine system

The internal system of chemical communication involving hormones, the ductless glands that secrete hormones, and the molecular receptors on or in target cells that respond to hormones; functions in concert with the nervous system to affect internal regulation and maintain homeostasis.

Endocytosis

The cellular uptake of macromolecules and particulate substances by localized regions of the plasma membrane that surround the substance and pinch off to form an intracellular vesicle.

Endoderm

The innermost of the three primary germ layers in animal embryos; lines the archenteron and gives rise to the liver, pancreas, lungs, and the lining of the digestive tract.

Endodermis

The innermost layer of the cortex in plant roots; a cylinder one cell thick that forms the boundary between the cortex and the stele.

Endogenous

Arising from internal structures or functional causes.

Endomembrane system

The collection of membranes inside and around a eukaryotic cell, related either through direct physical contact or by the transfer of membranous vesicles.

Endometrium

The inner lining of the uterus, which is richly supplied with blood vessels.

Endonucleases

Endonucleases are enzymes that cleave the phosphodiester bond within a polynucleotide chain.

Endoparasites

A parasite, such as a tapeworm, that lives within another organism.

Endoplasmic reticulum

An extensive membranous network in eukaryotic cells, continuous with the outer nuclear membrane and composed of ribosome-studded (rough) and ribosome-free (smooth) regions.

Endorphin

A hormone produced in the brain and anterior pituitary that inhibits pain perception.

Endoskeleton

A hard skeleton buried within the soft tissues of an animal, such as the spicules of sponges, the plates of echinoderms, and the bony skeletons of vertebrates.

Endosperm

A nutrient-rich tissue formed by the union of a sperm cell with two polar nuclei during double fertilization, which provides nourishment to the developing embryo in angiosperm seeds.

Endospore

A thick-coated, resistant cell produced within a bacterial cell exposed to harsh conditions.

Endosymbiotic theory

A hypothesis about the origin of the eukaryotic cell, maintaining that the forerunners of eukaryotic cells were symbiotic associations of prokaryotic cells living inside larger prokaryotes.

Endothermic

Relating to a chemical reaction that absorbs heat.

Endothelium

The innermost, simple squamous layer of cells lining the blood vessels; the only constituent structure of capillaries.

Endotherm

An animal that uses metabolic energy to maintain a constant body temperature, such as a bird or mammal.

Endotoxin

A component of the outer membranes of certain gram-negative bacteria responsible for generalized symptoms of fever and ache.

Energy

The capacity to do work by moving matter against an opposing force.

Energy of activation

The amount of energy that reactants must absorb before a chemical reaction will start.

Enzymes

Any of several complex proteins that are produced by cells and act as catalysts in specific biochemical reactions. There are over 700 identified human enzymes.

Enhancer

A DNA sequence that recognizes certain transcription factors that can stimulate the transcription of nearby genes.

Entropy

A quantitative measure of disorder or randomness, symbolized by S.

Environmental grain

An ecological term for the effect of spatial variation, or patchiness, relative to the size and behaviour of an organism.

Enzyme

A class of proteins serving as catalysts, chemical agents that change the rate of a reaction without being consumed by the reaction.

Eocene

Belonging to the geologic time, rock series, or sedimentary deposits of the second epoch of the Tertiary Period, characterized by warm climates and the rise of most modern mammalian families.

Eoplasts

Any of several pigmented cytoplasmic organelles found in plant cells and other organisms, having various physiological functions, such as the synthesis and storage of food.

Epiblast

The outer layer of a blastula that gives rise to the ectoderm after gastrulation.

Epiblema

The epidermal cells of rootlets specially adapted to absorb liquids. *Goodale.*

Epicuticular waxes

The epicuticle is the outermost portion of the exoskeleton of an insect (and various other arthropods); its exact composition and structure may differ somewhat among different taxa, but certain aspects can be generalized:

It is secreted by the epidermis and is deposited on top of the procuticle via pores that pass outwards through the procuticle from the epidermal cells.

Epidermis

(1)   The dermal tissue system in plants.

(2)   The outer covering of animals.

Epidermal

about the epidermis; epidermic; cuticular.

Epigenesis

The progressive development of form in an embryo.

Epididymis

A long coiled tube into which sperm pass from the testis and are stored until mature and ejaculated.

Epigenesis

A cartilaginous flap that blocks the top of the windpipe, the glottis, during swallowing, which prevents the entry of food or fluid into the respiratory system.

Epigynous

Having a floral part (such as the petals and stamens) attached to or near the upper part of the ovary, as in the flower of the apple, cucumber, or daffodil.

Epinephrine

A hormone produced as a response to stress; also called adrenaline.

Epipetalous

Borne on or attached to the petals or corolla, as the stamens of the petunia.

Epiphyllous

Growing upon, or inserted into, the leaf.

Epiphyte

A plant that nourishes itself but grows on the surface of another plant for support, usually on the branches or trunks of tropical trees.

Episome

A plasmid capable of integrating into the bacterial chromosome.

Epistasis

A phenomenon in which one gene alters the expression of another gene that is independently inherited.

Epithelium

A cellular tissue covering the external and internal surfaces of the body.

Epithelial tissue

Sheets of tightly packed cells that line organs and body cavities.

Epitope

A localized region on the surface of an antigen that is chemically recognized by antibodies; also called the antigenic determinant.

Equilibrium

The state of a system in which no further net change is occurring; result of counterbalancing forward and backward processes.

Equilibrium species

Species characterized by low reproduction rates, long development times, large body size, and long adult life with repeated reproductions.

Equational division

Nuclear division in which each chromosome divides into equal longitudinal halves.

Equatorial plate

The plane located midway between the poles of a dividing cell during the metaphase stage of mitosis or meiosis. It is formed from the migration of the chromosomes to the centre of the spindle

Ergastic substances

Ergastic substances are non-protoplasm materials found in cells.

Ergot

The disease caused by such a fungus.

ER membranes

In eukaryotes, the functional continuum of membraneous cell components consisting of the nuclear envelope, endoplasmic reticulum, and Golgi apparatus as well as vesicles and other structures derived from these major components.

Ergastic substances

Ergastic substances are non-protoplasm materials found in cells. The living protoplasm of a cell is sometimes called the bioplasm and distinct from the orgastic substances of the cell.

Erythrocyte

A red blood cell; contains haemoglobin, which functions in transporting oxygen in the circulatory system.

Oesophagus

A channel that conducts food, by peristalsis, from the pharynx to the stomach.

Essential amino acids

The amino acids that an animal cannot synthesize itself and must obtain from food. Eight amino acids are essential in the human adult.

Esterification

A chemical reaction resulting in the formation of at least one ester product.

Estivation

A physiological state characterized by slow metabolism and inactivity, which permits survival during long periods of elevated temperature and diminished water supplies.

Estrogens

The primary female steroid sex hormones, which are produced in the ovary by the developing follicle during the first half of the cycle and in smaller quantities by the corpus luteum during the second half. Estrogens stimulate the development and maintenance of the female reproductive system and secondary sex characteristics.

Oestrous cycle

A type of reproductive cycle in all-female mammals except for higher primates, in which the nonpregnant endometrium is reabsorbed rather than shed, and sexual response occurs only during midcycle at estrus.

Ethology

The comparative study of patterns of animal behaviour, with emphasis on their adaptive significance and evolutionary origin.

Ethylene

The only gaseous plant hormone, responsible for fruit ripening, growth inhibition, leaf abscission, and ageing.

Etiolation

In plants, a condition characterized by stem elongation, poor leaf development, and lack of chlorophyll; occurs in plants growing in the dark or with greatly reduced light.

Etioplasts

Etioplasts are chloroplasts that have not been exposed to light. They are usually found in plants grown in the dark. If a plant is kept out of light for several days, its normal chloroplasts will convert into etioplasts.

Euchromatin

The more open, unravelled form of eukaryotic chromatin, which is available for transcription.

Eukaryotic cells

A type of cell with a membrane-enclosed nucleus and membrane-enclosed organelles, present in protists, plants, fungi, and animals; also called eukaryote.

Eukaryote

An organism whose cells contain membrane-bound organelles and whose DNA is enclosed in a cell nucleus and is associated with proteins.

Eumetazoa

Members of the subkingdom that includes all animals except sponges.

Eusocial

Applied to animal societies, such as those of certain insects, in which sterile individuals work on behalf of reproductive individuals.

Eutherian mammals

Placental mammals; those whose young complete their embryonic development within the uterus, joined to the mother by the placenta.

Eutrophic lake

A highly productive lake, having a high rate of biological productivity supported by a high rate of nutrient cycling.

Eutrophication

A process in which an aquatic environment accumulates high nutrient levels due to factors such as industrial or urban pollution or run-off of fertilizers from nearby agricultural lands. The nutrients lead to dense blooms of algae and aquatic plants that cloud lake water, deplete specific minerals and dissolved gases, and can cause natural plant and animal populations to decline.

Evaporative cooling

The property of a liquid whereby the surface becomes cooler during evaporation, owing to a loss of highly kinetic molecules to the gaseous state.

Evolution

All the changes that have transformed life on Earth from its earliest beginnings to the diversity that characterizes it today.

Evolutionary species concept

The idea that evolutionary lineages and ecological roles can form the basis of species identification.

Exaptation

A structure that evolves and functions in one environmental context but that can perform additional functions when placed in some new environment.

Excitatory postsynaptic potential (EPSP)

An electrical change (depolarization) in the membrane of a postsynaptic neuron caused by the binding of an excitatory neurotransmitter from a presynaptic cell to a postsynaptic receptor; makes it more likely for a postsynaptic neuron to generate an action potential.

Excretion

The disposal of nitrogen-containing waste products of metabolism.

Excretory

Of, relating to, or used in excretion: *excretory organs*.

Excretory organs

An organ that separates waste substances from the blood and discharges them.

Excretory system

The organ system that disposes of nitrogen-containing metabolic wastes.

Exergonic reaction

A spontaneous chemical reaction in which there is a net release of free energy.

Exocrine glands

Glands, such as sweat glands and digestive glands, that secrete their products into ducts that empty onto surfaces, such as the skin, or into cavities, such as the interior of the stomach.

Exocytosis

The cellular secretion of macromolecules by the fusion of vesicles with the plasma membrane.

Exodermis

A layer of cells lying immediately below the epidermis.

Exon

The coding region of a eukaryotic gene that is expressed. Exons are separated from each other by introns.

Exoskeleton

A hard encasement on the surface of an animal, such as the shells of molluscs or the cuticles of arthropods, that provides protection and points of attachment for muscles.

Exotoxin

A toxic protein secreted by a bacterial cell that produces specific symptoms even in the absence of the bacterium.

Exothermic

Relating to a chemical reaction that releases heat.

Exponential growth

In populations, the increasingly accelerated rate of growth due to the increasing number of individuals being added to the reproductive base. Exponential growth is very seldom approached or sustained in natural populations.

Expression vector

A vector that allows a DNA sequence cloned into it to be transcribed when the vector is introduced into a cell.

Expressivity

In genetics, the degree to which a particular genotype is expressed in the phenotype of individuals with that genotype.

Extinct

No longer existing.

Extracellular

Located or occurring outside a cell or cells.

Extracellular matrix (ECM)

The substance in which animal tissue cells are embedded; consists of protein and polysaccharides.

Extraembryonic membranes

Four membranes (yolk sac, amnion, chorion, allantois) that support the developing embryo in reptiles, birds, and mammals.

External morphology

The branch of biology that deals with the form and structure of an organism or part, without regard to function.

Eyelashes

Any of the short curved hairs that grow from the edges of the eyelids.

F

F_1 (first filial generation)

The first filial or hybrid offspring in a genetic cross-fertilization.

F_2 (second filial generation)

Offspring resulting from the interbreeding of the hybrid F_1 generation.

F factor

A fertility factor in bacteria, a DNA segment that confers the ability to form pili for conjugation and associated functions required for the transfer of DNA from donor to recipient. May exist as a plasmid or integrated into the bacterial chromosome.

Fascia

A sheet or band of fibrous connective tissue separating or binding together muscles and organs etc

Facilitated diffusion

The spontaneous passage of molecules and ions, bound to specific carrier proteins, across a biological membrane down their concentration gradients.

Facultative anaerobe

An organism that makes ATP by aerobic respiration if oxygen is present but that switches to fermentation under anaerobic conditions.

Fascicular cambium

Fascicular cambium (plant anatomy), ...vascular bundle develops a meristematic area of growth from an undifferentiated (parenchymatous) layer of cells between the primary xylem and primary phloem, called a fascicular cambium.

Fascicular vascular cambium

Cambium that develops within the vascular bundle.

FAD

Abbreviation of flavin adenine dinucleotide, a coenzyme that functions as an electron acceptor in the Krebs cycle.

Fallopian tube

Either of a pair of slender ducts through which ova pass from the ovaries to the uterus in the female reproductive system of humans and higher mammals.

Family

A taxonomic grouping of related, similar genera; the category below order and above genus.

Fat

A biological compound consisting of three fatty acids linked to one glycerol molecule.

Fatty acid

A long carbon chain carboxylic acid. Fatty acids vary in length and the number and location of double bonds; three fatty acids linked to a glycerol molecule form fat.

Feedback inhibition

A method of metabolic control in which the end-product of a metabolic pathway acts as an inhibitor of an enzyme within that pathway.

Feedback systems

Control mechanisms whereby an increase or decrease in the level of a particular factor inhibits or stimulates the production, utilization, or release of that factor; important in the regulation of enzyme and hormone levels, ion concentrations, temperature, and many other factors.

Fermentation

A catabolic process that makes a limited amount of ATP from glucose without an electron transport chain and that produces a characteristic end-product, such as ethyl alcohol or lactic acid.

Fertilization

The union of haploid gametes to produce a diploid zygote.

Fetal membrane

Any of the membranous structures closely associated with or surrounding a developing vertebrate embryo, including the amnion, chorion, allantois, and yolk sac.

Fetus

An unborn or unhatched vertebrate that has passed through the earliest developmental stages; a developing human from about the second month of gestation until birth.

Fibre

A lignified cell type that reinforces the xylem of angiosperms and functions in mechanical support; a slender, tapered sclerenchyma cell that usually occurs in bundles.

Fibril

Any minute, threadlike structure within a cell.

Fibrin

The activated form of the blood-clotting protein fibrinogen, which aggregates into threads that form the fabric of the clot.

Fibrillin

Fibrillin is a glycoprotein, which is essential for the formation of elastic fibres found in connective tissue.

Fibroin

Fibroin is a type of protein created by silkworms in the production of silk.

Fibroblast

A type of cell in loose connective tissue that secretes the protein ingredients of the extracellular fibres.

Fibrous protein

Insoluble structural protein in which the polypeptide chain is coiled along one dimension. Fibrous proteins constitute the main structural elements of many animal tissues.

Fibula

The outer and narrower of two bones of the human lower leg, extending from the knee to the ankle.

Filament

A chain of cells.

Filtrate

Fluid extracted by the excretory system from the blood or body cavity. The excretory system produces urine from the filtrate after extracting valuable solutes from it and concentrating it.

Filtration

The first stage of kidney function; blood plasma is forced, under pressure, out of the glomerular capillaries into Bowman's capsule, through which it enters the renal tubule.

Fimbriae

A fringelike anatomical part or structure.

The first law of thermodynamics

The principle of conservation of energy. Energy can be transferred and transformed, but it cannot be created or destroyed.

Fitness

The genetic contribution of an individual to succeeding generations relative to the contributions of other individuals in the population.

Fixed action pattern

A highly stereotypical behaviour that is innate and must be carried to completion once initiated.

Flaccid

Limp; walled cells are flaccid in isotonic surroundings, where there is no tendency for water to enter.

Flagellum

A long cellular appendage specialized for locomotion, formed from a core of nine outer doublet microtubules and two inner single microtubules, ensheathed in an extension of the plasma membrane.

Flame cells

the organ of excretion in flatworms

Flatworms

Any of various parasitic and nonparasitic worms of the phylum Platyhelminthes, such as a tapeworm or a planarian, characteristically having a soft, flat, bilaterally symmetrical body and no body cavity. Also called *platyhelminth*.

Flower

The reproductive structure of angiosperms; a complete flower includes sepals, petals, stamens (male structures), and carpels (female structures).

Fluid-feeder

An animal that lives by sucking nutrient-rich fluids from another living organism.

Fluid mosaic model

The currently accepted model of cell membrane structure, which envisions the membrane as a mosaic of individually inserted protein molecules drifting laterally in a fluid bilayer of phospholipids.

Follicle

A microscopic structure in the ovary that contains the developing ovum and secretes estrogens.

Follicle-stimulating hormone (FSH)

A protein hormone secreted by the anterior pituitary that stimulates the production of eggs by the ovaries and sperm by the testes.

Fontana

A city of southern California west of San Bernardino. It is an industrial centre in a citrus- growing area. Population: 170,000.

Food chain

The pathway along which food is transferred from trophic level to trophic level, beginning with producers.

Food web

The elaborate, interconnected feeding relationships in an ecosystem.

Foregut

The anterior alimentary canal in a vertebrate embryo, including those parts which will develop into the pharynx, oesophagus, stomach, and anterior intestine.

Fossil

The remains of an organism, or direct evidence of its presence (such as tracks). Maybe an unaltered hard part (tooth or bone), a mould in a rock, petrification (wood or bone), unaltered or partially altered soft parts (a frozen mammoth).

Founder effect

A cause of genetic drift attributable to colonization by a limited number of individuals from a parent population.

Fovea

A small area in the centre of the retina in which cones are concentrated; the area of sharpest vision.

Fragile X syndrome

A hereditary mental disorder, partially explained by genomic imprinting and the addition of nucleotides to a triplet repeat near the end of an X chromosome.

Fragmentation

A method of asexual reproduction, occurring in some invertebrate animals, in which parts of the organism break of and subsequently differentiate and develop and new individuals. It occurs, especially in certain coelenterates and annelids.

Frameshift mutation

A mutation occurring when the number of nucleotides inserted or deleted is not a multiple of 3, thus resulting in improper grouping into codons.

Free energy

A quantity of energy that interrelates entropy (S) and the system's total energy (H); symbolized by G. The change in free energy of a system is calculated by the equation $G = \Delta H$

$- T \Delta S$, where T is the absolute temperature.

Free energy of activation

The initial investment of energy necessary to start a chemical reaction; also called activation energy.

Frequency-dependent selection

A decline in the reproductive success of a morph resulting from the morph's phenotype becoming too common in a population; a cause of balanced polymorphism in populations.

Fungi

A group of simple plants lacking chlorophyll.

Fruit

A mature ovary of a flower that protects dormant seeds and aids in their dispersal.

Function

Characteristic role or action of a structure or process in the normal metabolism or behaviour of an organism.

Functional group

A specific configuration of atoms commonly attached to the carbon skeletons of organic molecules and usually involved in chemical reactions.

G

Gases

An aeriform fluid that possesses complete molecular mobility and the property of indefinite expansion. A gas has no definite shape, and its volume is determined by its container and by temperature and pressure.

G protein

A GTP-binding protein that relays signals from a plasma-membrane signal receptor, known as a G-protein linked receptor, to other signal-transduction proteins inside the cell. When such a receptor is activated, it, in turn, activates the G protein, causing it to bind a molecule of GTP in place of GDP. Hydrolysis of the bound GTP to GDP inactivates the G protein.

G-protein linked receptor

A signal receptor protein in the plasma membrane that responds to the binding of a signal molecule by activating a G protein.

G_0 Phase

The G_0 phase (G sub 0) or *G zero* is a period in the cell cycle where cells exist in a quiescent state. G_0 is sometimes referred to as a "post-mitotic" state since cells in G_0 are in a non-dividing phase outside of the cell cycle;

G_1 phase

The first growth phase of the cell cycle, consisting of the portion of interphase before DNA synthesis begins.

G_2 phase

The second growth phase of the cell cycle, consisting of the portion of interphase after DNA synthesis occurs.

Gallbladder

A small, pear-shaped muscular sac, located under the right lobe of the liver, in which bile secreted by the liver is stored until needed by the body for digestion.

Golgi apparatus

The Golgi apparatus is an organelle found in most eukaryotic cells. It was identified in 1898 by the Italian physician Camillo Golgi and was named after him.

Gametangium

The reproductive organ of bryophytes, consisting of the male antheridium and female archegonium; a multichambered jacket of sterile cells in which gametes are formed.   An organ or a cell in which gametes are produced.## Gamete

A haploid egg or sperm cell; gametes unite during sexual reproduction to produce a diploid zygote.

Gametophyte

The multicellular haploid form in organisms undergoing alternation of generations, which mitotically produces haploid gametes that unite and grow into the sporophyte generation.

Ganglion

A cluster (functional group) of nerve cell bodies in a centralized nervous system.

Gap junction

A type of intercellular junction in animal cells that allows the passage of material or current between cells.

Gap phases

In the cell cycle, the phases that precede (G_1) and follow (G_2) the synthesis (S) phase in which DNA is replicated; in the G_1 phase, the cell doubles in size, and its enzymes, ribosomes, and other cytoplasmic molecules and structures increase in number; in the G_2 phase, the replicated chromosomes begin to condense and the structures required for mitosis or meiosis are assembled.

Gastric

About the stomach.

Gastrin

A digestive hormone, secreted by the stomach, that stimulates the secretion of gastric juice.

Gastrodermis

The cellular lining of the digestive cavity of certain invertebrates.

Gastrotricha

Any of various minute aquatic animals of the phylum Gastrotricha, having a wormlike, ciliated body.

Gastrovascular

Having both a digestive and a circulatory function. Used especially to describe the body cavity of a coelenterate.

Gastrovascular cavity

The central digestive compartment, usually with a single opening that functions as both mouth and anus.

Gastrula

The two-layered, cup-shaped embryonic stage.

Gastrulation

The formation of a gastrula from a blastula.

Gated ion channel

A specific ion channel that opens and closes to allow the cell to alter its membrane potential.

Principle

Any original inherent constituent which characterizes a substance, or gives it its essential properties, and which can usually be separated by analysis; -- applied especially to drugs, plant extracts, etc.

Gel electrophoresis

The separation of nucleic acids or proteins, based on their size and electrical charge, by measuring their rate of movement through an electrical field in a gel.

Gene

A discrete unit of hereditary information consisting of a specific nucleotide sequence in DNA (or RNA, in some viruses).

Gene amplification

The selective synthesis of DNA, which results in multiple copies of a single gene, thereby enhancing expression.

Gene cloning

The production of multiple copies of a gene.

Gene flow

The loss or gain of alleles from a population due to the emigration or immigration of fertile individuals, or the transfer of gametes, between populations.

Gene pool

The total aggregate of genes in a population at any one time.

Genetic code

The system of nucleotide triplets in DNA and RNA that carries genetic information; referred to as a code because it determines the amino acid sequence in the enzymes and other protein molecules synthesized by the organism.

Genetic drift

Changes in the gene pool of a small population due to chance.

Genetic information

The total accumulation of known genetic data on all organisms. The term may also be applied to individuals or families, i.e., the total is known as genetic data for a given person or family group.

Genetic isolation

The absence of genetic exchange between populations or species as a result of geographic separation or of premating or postmating mechanisms (behavioural, anatomical, or physiological) that prevent reproduction.

Genetic map

An ordered list of genetic loci (genes or other genetic markers) along a chromosome.

Genetic recombination

The general term for the production of offspring that combine traits of the two parents.

Ganoid

Primitive fishes having thick bony scales with a shiny covering

Genome

The complete complement of an organism's genes; an organism's genetic material.

Genomic imprinting

The parental effect on gene expression. Identical alleles may have different effects on offspring, depending on whether they arrive in the zygote via the ovum or via the sperm.

Genomic library

A set of thousands of DNA segments from a genome, each carried by a plasmid, phage, or another cloning vector.

Gene mutations

A mutation due to an intramolecular reorganization of a gene.

Genotype

The genetic makeup of an organism.

Genus

A taxonomic category above the species level, designated by the first word of a species' binomial Latin name.

Geographical range

The geographic area in which a population lives.

Geological time scale

A time scale established by geologists that reflects a consistent sequence of historical periods, grouped into four eras: Precambrian, Paleozoic, Mesozoic, and Cenozoic.

Germ cells

Gametes or the cells that give rise to gametes.

Germarium

The egg-producing portion of an ovary and the sperm-producing portion of testis in Platyhelminthes and Rotifera.

Germination

In plants, the resumption of growth or the development from seed or spore.

Germplasm

Germplasm is a collection of genetic resources for an organism

Gibberellin

A class of related plant hormones that stimulate growth in the stem and leaves, trigger the germination of seeds and breaking of bud dormancy and stimulate fruit development with auxin.

Gill

A localized extension of the body surface of many aquatic animals specialized for gas exchange.

Gland

A structure composed of modified epithelial cells specialized to produce one or more secretions that are discharged to the outside of the gland.

Glandular

Relating to, affecting, or resembling a gland or its secretion.

Glial cell

A nonconducting cell of the nervous system that provides support, insulation, and protection for the neurons.

Globular protein

A polypeptide chain folded into a roughly spherical shape.

Golgi apparatus

(*Cell and molecular biology*) A cellular organelle that is part of the cytoplasmic membrane system; it is composed of regions of stacked cisternae and it functions in secretory processes.

Glomerulus

A ball of capillaries surrounded by Bowman's capsule in the nephron and serving as the site of filtration in the vertebrate kidney.

Glottis

The opening between the vocal cords at the upper part of the larynx.

Glucagon

A peptide hormone secreted by pancreatic endocrine cells that raises blood glucose levels; an antagonistic hormone to insulin.

Glucocorticoid

A corticosteroid hormone secreted by the adrenal cortex that influences glucose metabolism and immune function.

Glucose

A six-carbon sugar ($C_6H_{12}O_6$); the most common monosaccharide in animals.

Glycerol

A three-carbon molecule with three hydroxyls ($\overline{OH}$) groups attached; a glycerol molecule can combine with three fatty acid molecules to form a fat or oil.

Glycine

A nonessential amino acid. Glycine is the simplest amino acid. *Chemical formula: $C_2H_5NO_2$*

Glycocalyx

A fuzzy coat on the outside of animal cells, made of sticky oligosaccharides.

Glycogen

An extensively branched glucose storage polysaccharide found in the liver and muscle of animals; the animal equivalent of starch.

Glycogenolysis

The biochemical breakdown of glycogen to glucose.

Glycolipids

Organic molecules similar in structure to fats, but in which a short carbohydrate chain rather than a fatty acid is attached to the third carbon of the glycerol molecule; as a result, the molecule has a hydrophilic "head" and a hydrophobic "tail." Glycolipids are important constituents of the plasma membrane and organelle membranes.

Glycolysis

The splitting of glucose into pyruvate. Glycolysis is the one metabolic pathway that occurs in all living cells, serving as the starting point for fermentation or aerobic respiration.

Glycoprotein

A protein with covalently attached carbohydrate.

Glyoxisomes/Microbodies

Glyoxisomes are a kind of Microbodies. They are mainly present in plants. They are required for the processing of food in the body.

Gnathostomata

Comprising all vertebrates with upper and lower jaws

Golgi apparatus

An organelle in eukaryotic cells consisting of stacks of flat membranous sacs that modify, store, and route products of the endoplasmic reticulum.

Golgi bodies

A network of stacked membranous vesicles present in most living cells that functions in the formation of secretions within the cell. Also called the *Golgi body, Golgi complex.*

Golgi vesicles

A network of stacked membranous vesicles present in most living cells that functions in the formation of secretions within the cell. Also called the *Golgi body, Golgi complex.*

Golgi vacuoles

A small cavity in the cytoplasm of a cell, bound by a single membrane and containing water, food, or metabolic waste.

Gonadotropins

Hormones that stimulate the activities of the testes and ovaries; a collective term for follicle-stimulating and luteinizing hormones.

Gonads

The male and female sex organs; the gamete-producing organs in most animals.

Graded potential

A local voltage change in a neuron membrane induced by stimulation of a neuron, with strength proportional to the strength of the stimulus and lasting about a millisecond.

Gradualism

A view of Earth's history that attributes the profound change to the cumulative product of slow but continuous processes.

Gram-negative bacteria

Gream-negative bacteria are those that do not retain crystal violet dye in the Gram staining protocol.

Gram stain

A staining method that distinguishes between two different kinds of bacterial cell walls.

Granum

A stacked portion of the thylakoid membrane in the chloroplast. Grana function in the light reactions of photosynthesis.

Gravid

In an advanced stage of pregnancy; "was big with child"; "was great with child"

Gravitropism

A response of a plant or animal about gravity.

Greenhouse effect

The warming of planet Earth due to the atmospheric accumulation of carbon dioxide, which absorbs infrared radiation and slows its escape from the irradiated Earth.

Gross primary productivity (GPP)

The total primary productivity of an ecosystem.

Gross productivity

A measure of the rate at which energy is assimilated by the organisms in a trophic level, a community, or an ecosystem.

Ground meristem

A primary meristem that gives rise to ground tissue in plants.

Ground tissue system or fundamental tissue

A tissue of mostly parenchyma cells that makes up the bulk of a young plant and fills the space between the dermal and vascular tissue systems.

Growth factors

A protein that must be present in the extracellular environment (culture medium or animal body) for the growth and normal development of certain types of cells.

Guard cell

A specialized epidermal plant cell that forms the boundaries of the stomata.

Guttation

The exudation of water droplets caused by root pressure in certain plants.

Gymnosperms

An avascular plant that bears naked seeds not enclosed in any specialized chambers.

Gynoecium

The female reproductive organs of a flower; the pistil or pistils considered as a group.

Gynoecia

The female reproductive organs of a flower considered as a group; the pistil or pistils. Compare androecium.

H

Habitat

The place in which individuals of a particular species can usually be found.

Habituation

A simple kind of learning involving a loss of sensitivity to unimportant stimuli, allowing an animal to conserve time and energy.

Half chordate

Hemichordates ("half chordates") have some features similar to those of chordates.

Half-life

The average time required for the disappearance or decay of one-half of any amount of a given substance.

Haploid cell

A cell containing only one set of chromosomes.

Hardy-Weinberg equilibrium

The steady-state relationship between relative frequencies of two or more alleles in an idealized population; both the allele frequencies and the genotype frequencies will remain constant from generation to generation in a population breeding at random in the absence of evolutionary forces.

Hardy-Weinberg theorem

An axiom maintaining that the sexual shuffling of genes alone cannot alter the overall genetic makeup of a population.

Haustorium

In parasitic fungi, a nutrient-absorbing hyphal tip that penetrates the tissues of the host but remains outside the host cell membranes.

Haversian system

One of many structural units of vertebrate bone, consisting of concentric layers of the mineralized bone matrix surrounding lacunae, which contain osteocytes, and a central canal, which contains blood vessels and nerves.

Heat

The total amount of kinetic energy due to molecular motion in a body of matter. Heat is energy in its most random form.

Heat of vaporization

The amount of heat required to change a given amount of a liquid into a gas; 540 calories are required to change 1 gram of liquid water into vapour.

Heat-shock protein

A protein that helps protect other proteins during heat stress, found in plants, animals, and microorganisms.

Helper T cell (T_H)

A type of T cell that is required by some B cells to help them make antibodies or that helps other T cells respond to antigens or secrete lymphokines or interleukins.

Heme

The iron-containing group of heme proteins such as haemoglobin and the cytochromes.

Hematopoietic system

The system in the body which is responsible for the production of blood cells.

Hemicelluloses

Any of several polysaccharides that are more complex than sugar and less complex than cellulose, found in plant cell walls and produced commercially from corn grain hulls.

Hemichordata

A group of marine animals categorized as either a phylum of deuterostomes or a subphylum of chordates; includes the Enteropneusta, Pterobranchia, and Graptolithina.

Haemoglobin

An iron-containing protein in red blood cells that reversibly binds oxygen.

Haemophilia

A group of hereditary disorders characterized by failure of the blood to clot and consequent excessive bleeding from even minor wounds.

Hemolymph

In invertebrates with an open circulatory system, the body fluid that bathes tissues.

Hepatic

About the liver.

Hepatic portal vessel

A large circulatory channel that conveys nutrient-laden blood from the small intestine to the liver, which regulates the blood's nutrient content.

Herbaceous

In plants, nonwoody.

Herbivore

A heterotrophic animal that eats plants.

Heredity

The transmission of characteristics from parent to offspring.

Hermaphrodite

An individual that functions as both male and female in sexual reproduction by producing both sperm and eggs.

Heterochromatin

Untranscribed eukaryotic chromatin that is so highly compacted that it is visible with a light microscope during interphase.

Heterochrony

Evolutionary changes in the timing or rate of development.

Heterocyst

A specialized cell that engages in nitrogen fixation on some filamentous cyanobacteria.

Hematopoietic system

The bodily system of organs and tissues, primarily the bone marrow, spleen, tonsils, and lymph nodes, involved in the production of blood.

Hemocoel

A hemocoel is a series of spaces between the organs of organisms with open circulatory systems, like most arthropods and molluscs

Heteromorphic

A condition in the life cycle of all modern plants in which the sporophyte and gametophyte generations differ in morphology.

Heterosporous

Referring to plants in which the sporophyte produces two kinds of spores that develop into unisexual gametophytes, either female or male.

Heterotroph

An organism that obtains organic food molecules by eating other organisms or their by-products.

Heterozygote

A diploid organism that carries two different alleles at one or more genetic loci.

Heterozygote advantage

A mechanism that preserves variation in eukaryotic gene pools by conferring greater reproductive success on heterozygotes over individuals homozygous for any one of the associated alleles.

Heterozygous

Having two different alleles for a given genetic character.

Hibernation

A physiological state that allows survival during long periods of cold temperatures and reduced food supplies, in which metabolism decreases, the heart and respiratory system slow down, and body temperature is maintained at a lower level than normal.

Hilum

The scar on a seed, such as a bean, indicating the point of attachment to the funiculus.

Hindgut

The caudal portion of the embryonic alimentary canal in vertebrates.

Histamine

A substance released by injured cells that causes blood vessels to dilate during an inflammatory response.

Histone

A small protein with a high proportion of positively charged amino acids that binds to the negatively charged DNA and plays a key role in its chromatin structure.

HIV

Abbreviation of human immunodeficiency virus, the infectious agent that causes AIDS; HIV is an RNA retrovirus.

Holoblastic cleavage

A type of cleavage in which there is a complete division of the egg, as in eggs having little yolk (sea urchin) or a moderate amount of yolk (frog).

Holozoic

Obtaining nourishment by the ingestion of organic material, as animals do.

Holophytic

An organism that produces its food through photosynthesis.

Hooks

A curved or sharply bent device, usually of metal, used to catch, drag, suspend, or fasten something else.

Homeobox

A 180-nucleotide sequence within a homeotic gene encoding the part of the protein that binds to the DNA of the genes regulated by the protein.

Homeosis

Evolutionary alteration in the placement of different body parts.

Homeostasis

The steady-state physiological condition of the body.

Homeotherm

An organism, such as a bird or mammal, capable of maintaining a stable body temperature independent of the environment.

Homeotic genes

Genes that control the overall body plan of animals by controlling the developmental fate of groups of cells.

Hominid

Humans and closely related primates; includes modern and fossil forms, such as the australopithecines, but not the apes.

Hominoid

Hominids and the apes.

Homodont

Vertebrate zoology

Homologous chromosomes

Chromosome pairs of the same length, centromere position, and staining pattern that possess genes for the same characters at corresponding loci. One homologous chromosome is inherited from the organism's father, the other from the mother.

Homologous structures

Structures in different species that are similar because of common ancestry.

Homology

The similarity in characteristics resulting from shared ancestry.

Homosporous

Referring to plants in which a single type of spore develops into a bisexual gametophyte having both male and female sex organs.

Homozygote

A diploid organism that carries identical alleles at one or more genetic loci.

Homozygous

Having two identical alleles for a given trait.

Hormone

One of many types of circulating chemical signals in all multicellular organisms that are formed in specialized cells, travel in body fluids and coordinate the various parts of the organism by interacting with target cells.

Host

An organism on or in which a parasite lives.

Human

The modern species of humans, the only extant species of the primate family Hominidae.

Human Genome Project

An international collaborative effort to map and sequence the DNA of the entire human genome.

Humerus

The long bone of the arm or forelimb, extending from the shoulder to the elbow.

Humoral immunity

The type of immunity that fights bacteria and viruses in body fluids with antibodies that circulate in blood plasma and lymph, fluids formerly called humour.

Hummingbird

Any of numerous New World birds of the family Trochilidae, usually very small in size and having brilliant iridescent plumage, a long slender bill, and wings capable of beating very rapidly, thereby enabling the bird to hover.

Hybrid

Offspring of two different varieties or two different species.

Hybrid zone

A region where two related populations that diverged after becoming geographically isolated make secondary contact and interbreed where their geographical ranges overlap.

Hydrocarbon

An organic molecule consisting only of carbon and hydrogen.

Hydrogen bond

A type of weak chemical bond formed when the slightly positive hydrogen atom of a polar covalent bond in one molecule is attracted to the slightly negative atom of a polar covalent bond in another molecule.

Hydrolysis

A chemical process that lyses or splits molecules by the addition of water; essential process indigestion.

Hydrogen ion

A single proton with a charge of +1. The dissociation of a water molecule (H_2O) leads to the generation of a hydroxide ion (OH^-) and a hydrogen ion (H^+).

Hydrophilic

Having an affinity for water.

Hydrophobic

Having an aversion to water; tending to coalesce and form droplets in water.

Hydrostatic skeleton

A skeletal system composed of fluid held under pressure in a closed body compartment; the main skeleton of most cnidarians, flatworms, nematodes, and annelids.

Hydroxyl group

A functional group consisting of a hydrogen atom joined to an oxygen atom by a polar covalent bond. Molecules possessing this group are soluble in water and are called alcohols.

Hyperpolarization

An electrical state whereby the inside of the cell is made more negative relative to the outside than at the resting membrane potential. A neuron membrane is hyperpolarized if a stimulus increases its voltage from the resting potential of -70 mV, reducing the chance that the neuron will transmit a nerve impulse.

Hypertonic solution

A solution with a greater solute concentration than another, a hypotonic solution.

Hypha

A filament that collectively makes up the body of a fungus.

Hypodermis

An epidermal layer of cells that secretes an overlying chitinous cuticle, as in arthropods.

Hypogynous

Having the floral parts, such as sepals, petals, and stamens, borne on the receptacle beneath the ovary.

Hypothalamus

The central part of the vertebrate forebrain; functions in maintaining homeostasis, especially in coordinating the endocrine and nervous systems; secretes hormones of the posterior pituitary and releasing factors, which regulate the anterior pituitary.

Hypothesis

A temporary working explanation or supposition based on accumulated facts and suggesting some general principle or relation of cause and effect; a postulated solution to a scientific problem that must be tested and if not validated, discarded.

Hypotonic solution

A solution with a lesser solute concentration than another, a hypertonic solution

Hypostomata

Having stomata (mostly) on the underneath

I

Ichthyologist

Biologists who specialize in the study of fish behaviour, anatomy, physiology, and evolution.

Ileum

The terminal portion of the small intestine extending from the jejunum to the cecum

Intracellular.

Occurring or situated within a cell or cells: intracellular fluid.

Intra-fascicular cambium

The cambium arising between the vascular bundles in the stem of a plant

Inner endodermis

The innermost layer of the cortex that forms a sheath around the vascular tissue of roots and some stems.

Imaginal disk

An island of undifferentiated cells in an insect larva, which are committed (determined) to form a particular organ during metamorphosis to the adult.

Imbibition

The capillary movement of water into germinating seeds and into substances such as wood and gelatin, which swell as a result.

Imbricate

Having regularly arranged, overlapping edges, like roof tiles or fish scales.

Immune response

A highly specific defensive reaction of the body to invasion by a foreign substance or organism; consists of a primary response in which the invader is recognized as foreign, or "not-self," and eliminated and a secondary response to subsequent attacks by the same invader. Mediated by two types of lymphocytes B cells, which mature in the bone marrow and are responsible for antibody production, and T cells, which mature in the thymus and are responsible for cell-mediated immunity.

Immune system

a system (including the thymus and bone marrow and lymphoid tissues) that protects the body from foreign substances and pathogenic organisms by producing the immune response.

Immunoglobulin (Ig)

One of the classes of proteins comprising the antibodies.

Imprinting

A type of learned behaviour with a significant innate component, acquired during a limited critical period.

Inbreeding

The mating of individuals that are closely related genetically.

Incisor

A tooth for cutting or gnawing; located in the front of the mouth in both jaws.

Inclusive fitness

The relative number of an individual's alleles that are passed on from generation to generation, either as a result of his or her reproductive success, or that of related individuals.

Incomplete dominance

A type of inheritance in which F_1 hybrids have an appearance that is intermediate between the phenotypes of the parental varieties.

Incomplete flower

A flower lacking sepals, petals, stamens, or carpels.

Incomplete metamorphosis

A type of development in certain insects, such as grasshoppers, in which the larvae resemble adults but are smaller and have different body proportions. The animal goes through a series of moults, each time looking more like an adult until it reaches full size.

Independent assortment

Formation of random combinations of chromosomes in meiosis and of genes on different pairs of homologous chromosomes by the passage at random of one of each diploid pair of homologous chromosomes into each gamete independently of each other pair.

Independent variable

In an experiment, when one factor is manipulated, a second factor responds. The independent variable is the factor that is manipulated.

Indeterminate cleavage

A type of embryonic development in deuterostomes, in which each cell produced by early cleavage divisions retains the capacity to develop into a complete embryo.

Indeterminate growth

A type of growth characteristic of plants, in which the organism continues to grow as long as it lives.

Induced fit

The change in the shape of the active site of an enzyme so that it binds more snugly to the substrate, induced by entry of the substrate.

Induction

(1)   The ability of one group of embryonic cells to influence the development of another.

(2)   In genetics, the phenomenon in which the presence of a substrate (the inducer) initiates transcription and translation of the genes coding for the enzymes required for its metabolism.

Inflammatory response

A line of defence triggered by penetration of the skin or mucous membranes, in which small blood vessels in the vicinity of an injury dilate and become leakier, enhancing the infiltration of leukocytes; may also be widespread in the body.

Ingestion

A heterotrophic mode of nutrition in which other organisms or detritus are eaten whole or in pieces.

Inhibitory postsynaptic potential (IPSP)

An electrical charge (hyperpolarization) in the membrane of a postsynaptic neuron caused by the binding of an inhibitory neurotransmitter from a presynaptic cell to a postsynaptic receptor; makes it more difficult for a postsynaptic neuron to generate an action potential. Innate releasing mechanism

In ethology, a circuit within an animal's brain that is hypothesized to respond to a specific stimulus, setting in motion, or "releasing," the sequence of movements that constitute a fixed action pattern.

Inner cell mass

A cluster of cells in a mammalian blastocyst that protrudes into one end of the cavity and subsequently develops into the embryo proper and some of the extraembryonic membranes.

Inositol trisphosphate (IP$_3$)

The second messenger, which functions as an intermediate between certain nonsteroid hormones and the third messenger, a rise in cytoplasmic Ca^{2+} concentration.

Insertion

A mutation involving the addition of one or more nucleotide pairs to a gene.

Insertion sequence

The simplest kind of a transposon, consisting of inverted repeats of DNA flanking a gene for transposase, the enzyme that catalyzes transposition.

Insight learning

The ability of an animal to perform a correct or appropriate behaviour on the first attempt in a situation with which it has had no prior experience.

Instar

The stage of an arthropod's life cycle between moults (shedding of the exoskeleton). As an example, the third instar is the stage of the life cycle between the second and third moulting cycles. Some arthropods moult throughout their entire life and may have as many as 30 instars. Insects tend to have a set number of instars, the number varying by species. The instars succeed one another until the final mature instar when the organism stops moulting.

Insulin

A vertebrate hormone that lowers blood glucose levels by promoting the uptake of glucose by most body cells and the synthesis and storage of glycogen in the liver; also stimulates protein and fat synthesis; secreted by endocrine cells of the pancreas called islets of Langerhans.

Insulators

A material such as glass or porcelain with negligible electrical or thermal conductivity.

Integument

Any natural protective covering, The envelope of an ovule.

Intercalary meristem

Type of meristem active in certain plants, especially grasses, is the intercalary meristem

Interferon

A chemical messenger of the immune system, produced by virus-infected cells and capable of helping other cells resist the virus.

Interleukin

Interleukin-1, a chemical regulator (cytokine) secreted by macrophages that have ingested a pathogen or foreign molecule and have bound with a helper T cell; stimulates T cells to grow and divide and elevates body temperature. Interleukin-2, secreted by activated T cells, stimulates helper T cells to proliferate more rapidly.

Intermediate filaments

A component of the cytoskeleton that includes all filaments intermediate in size between microtubules and microfilaments.

Interneuron

An association neuron; a nerve cell within the central nervous system that forms synapses with sensory and motor neurons and integrates sensory input and motor output.

Internode

The segment of a plant stem between the points where leaves are attached.

Interphase

The period in the cell cycle when the cell is not dividing. During interphase, cellular metabolic activity is high, chromosomes and organelles are duplicated, and cell size may increase. Interphase accounts for 90% of the time of each cell cycle.

Interstitial cells

Cells scattered among the seminiferous tubules of the vertebrate testis that secrete testosterone and other androgens, the male sex hormones.

Interstitial fluid

The internal environment of vertebrates, consisting of the fluid filling the spaces between cells.

Intertidal zone

The shallow zone of the ocean where land meets water.

Intracellular

Occurring or situated within a cell or cells.

Intraembryonic

Within the embryo.

Interfascicular cambium

The cambium arising between the vascular bundles.

The intrinsic rate of increase

The difference between the number of births and the number of deaths, symbolized as $_{max}$; the maximum population growth rate.

Introgression

The transplantation of genes between species resulting from fertile hybrids mating successfully with one of the parent species.

Intron

A noncoding, intervening sequence within a eukaryotic gene.

Invagination

The local infolding of a layer of tissue, especially in animal embryos, to form a depression or pocket opening to the outside.

Interventricular septum

The muscular wall between the heart ventricles. Also known as ventricular septum.

Inversion

An aberration in chromosome structure resulting from an error in meiosis or from mutagens; reattachment in a reverse orientation of a chromosomal fragment to the chromosome from which the fragment originated.

Invertebrate

An animal without a backbone; invertebrates make up 95% of animal species.

In vitro fertilization

fertilization of ova in laboratory containers followed by artificial implantation of the early embryo in the mother's uterus.

Ion

an atom that has gained or lost electrons, thus acquiring a charge.

Ionic bond

A chemical bond resulting from the attraction between oppositely charged ions.

isogamy

A condition in which male and female gametes are morphologically indistinguishable.

Isolating mechanisms

Mechanisms that prevent genetic exchange between individuals of different populations or species; they prevent mating or successful reproduction even when mating occurs; maybe behavioural, anatomical, or physiological.

Isomerism

The complex of chemical and physical phenomena characteristic of or attributable to isomers.

Isomer

One of several organic compounds with the same molecular formula but different structures and therefore different properties. The three types are structural isomers, geometric isomers, and enantiomers.

Isomorphic generations

Alternating generations in which the sporophytes and gametophytes look alike, although they differ in chromosome number.

Isotonic solution

Solutions of equal solute concentration.

Isotope

One of several atomic forms of an element, each containing a different number of neutrons and thus differing in atomic mass.

J

Jaws

Either of two bony or cartilaginous structures that in most vertebrates form the framework of the mouth and hold the teeth.

"Junk" DNA

Stretches of DNA that do not code for genes; "most of the genome consists of junk DNA".

Joule (J)

A unit of energy: 1 J = 0.239 cal; 1 cal = 4.184 J.

Juvenile hormone (JH)

A hormone in arthropods, secreted by the corpora allata glands, that promotes the retention of larval characteristics.

Juxtaglomerular apparatus (JGA)

Specialized tissue located near the afferent arteriole that supplies blood to the kidney glomerulus; the JGA raises blood pressure by producing renin, which activates angiotensin.

K

K-selection

The concept that in certain (K-selected) populations, life history is centred around producing relatively few offspring that have a good chance of survival.

Karyogamy

The fusion of nuclei of two cells, as part of syngamy.

Karyokinesis

Division of the nucleus during the cell cycle.

Karyotype

A method of organizing the chromosomes of a cell about number, size, and type.

Kelp

Any of various brown, often very large seaweeds of the order Laminariales.

Keratin

One of a group of tough, fibrous proteins formed by certain epidermal tissues and especially abundant in skin, claws, hair, feathers, and hooves.

Keystone predator

A predatory species that help maintain species richness in a community by reducing the density of populations of the best competitors so that populations of less competitive species are maintained.

Keystone species

A species that is of exceptional importance in maintaining the species diversity of a community; when a keystone species is lost, the diversity of the community decreases and its structure is significantly altered.

Kidney

Invertebrates, the organ that regulates the balance of water and solutes in the blood and the excretion of nitrogenous wastes in the form of urine.

Kilobase

A unit of information equal to 1000 bits

Kilocalorie (kcal)

A thousand calories; the amount of heat energy required to raise the temperature of 1 kg of water 1°C.

Kin selection

A phenomenon of inclusive fitness used to explain altruistic behaviour between related individuals.

Kinesis

A change in activity rate in response to a stimulus.

Kinetic energy

The energy of motion, which is directly related to the speed of that motion. Moving matter does work by transferring some of its kinetic energy to other matter.

Kinetochores

A specialized region on the centromere that links each sister chromatid to the mitotic spindle.

Kingdom

A taxonomic category, the second broadest after the domain.

Koch's postulates

A set of four criteria for determining whether a specific pathogen is the cause of a disease.

Krebs cycle

A chemical cycle involving eight steps that completes the metabolic breakdown of glucose molecules to carbon dioxide; occurs within the mitochondrion; the second major stage in cellular respiration.

L

Lacteal

A tiny lymph vessel extending into the core of an intestinal villus and serving as the destination for absorbed chylomicrons.

Lagging strand

A discontinuously synthesized DNA strand that elongates in a direction away from the replication fork.

Lamella

Layer, thin sheet.

Lamina

A thin plate or layer (especially of bone or mineral).

Larva

A free-living, sexually immature form in some animal life cycles that may differ from the adult in morphology, nutrition, and habitat.

Lateral line system

A mechanoreceptor system consisting of a series of pores and receptor units (neuromasts) along the sides of the body of fishes and aquatic amphibians; detects water movements made by an animal itself and by other moving objects.

Lateral meristem or seconadary meristem

The vascular and cork cambium, a cylinder of dividing cells that runs most of the length of stems and roots and is responsible for secondary growth.

Latex

The colourless or milky sap of certain trees and plants, such as the milkweed and the rubber tree, that hardens when exposed to the air. Latex usually contains gum resins, waxes, and oils, and sometimes toxic substances.

Law of independent assortment

Mendel's second law, stating that each allele pair segregates independently during gamete formation; applies when genes for two traits are located on different pairs of homologous chromosomes.

Law of segregation

Mendel's first law, stating that allele pairs separate during gamete formation, and then randomly re-form pairs during the fusion of gametes at fertilization.

Leaching

The dissolving of minerals and other elements in soil or rocks by the downward movement of water.

Leading strand

The new continuous complementary DNA strand synthesized along the template strand in the mandatory 5' to 3' direction.

Leaf

The main site of photosynthesis in a plant; consists of a flattened blade and a stalk (petiole) that joins the leaf to the stem.

Leaping

The act of leaping; a jump.

Learning

The process that leads to modification in individual behaviour as a result of experience.

Left atrium

The left upper chamber of the heart that receives blood from the pulmonary veins.

Leptotene

The first stage of the prophase of meiosis.

Leukocyte

A white blood cell; typically functions in immunity, such as phagocytosis or antibody production.

Leukotriene

A type of prostaglandin produced by various white blood cells involved in the inflammatory and immune responses and allergic reactions.

Lichen

An organism formed by the symbiotic association between a fungus and a photosynthetic alga.

Life cycle

The entire sequence of stages in the life of an organism, from the adults of one generation to the adults of the next.

Life-history pattern

A group of traits, such as size and number of offspring, length of maturation, age at first reproduction, and the number of times reproduction occurs, that affect reproduction, survival, and the rate of population growth.

Life table

A table of data summarizing mortality in a population.

Ligament

A type of fibrous connective tissue that joins bones together at joints.

Ligand

A molecule that binds specifically to a receptor site of another molecule.

Ligand-gated ion channel receptor

A signal receptor protein in a cell membrane that can act as a channel for the passage of a specific ion across the membrane. When activated by a signal molecule, the receptor either allows or blocks the passage of the ion, resulting in a change in ion concentration that usually affects cell functioning.

Light-dependent reactions

The reactions of the first stage of photosynthesis, in which light energy is captured by chlorophyll molecules and converted to chemical energy stored in ATP and NADPH molecules.

Light-independent reactions

The carbon-fixing reactions of the second stage of photosynthesis; energy stored in ATP and NADPH by the light-dependent reactions is used to reduce carbon from carbon dioxide to simple sugars; light is not required for these reactions.

Ligament

A sheet or band of tough, fibrous tissue connecting bones or cartilages at a joint or supporting an organ.

Light microscope (LM)

An optical instrument with lenses that refract (bend) visible light to magnify images of specimens.

Light reactions

The steps in photosynthesis that occur on the thylakoid membranes of the chloroplast and convert solar energy to the chemical energy of ATP and NADPH, evolving oxygen in the process.

Lignin

A hard material embedded in the cellulose matrix of vascular plant cell walls that functions as an important adaptation for support in terrestrial species.

Limbic system

A group of nuclei (clusters of nerve cell bodies) in the lower part of the mammalian forebrain that interact with the cerebral cortex in determining emotions; includes the hippocampus and the amygdala.

Lymphatic systems

The interconnected system of spaces and vessels between body tissues and organs by which lymph circulates throughout the body.

Linkage

The tendency for certain alleles to be inherited together because they are located on the same chromosome.

Linked genes

Genes that are located on the same chromosome.

Linkage group

A pair of homologous chromosomes.

Linkage map

A genetic map based on the frequencies of recombination between markers during crossing over of homologous chromosomes. The greater the frequency of recombination between two genetic markers, the farther apart they are assumed to be.

Lipid

One of a family of compounds, including fats, phospholipids, and steroids, that are insoluble in water.

Lipochondria / idiosomes

Temporary storage vacuoles of lipids found in the Golgi apparatus.

Lipoprotein

A protein bonded to a lipid; includes the low-density lipoproteins (LDLs) and high-density lipoproteins (HDLs) that transport fats and cholesterol in the blood.

Lipopolysaccharides

Lipopolysaccharide is a large molecule consisting of a lipid and a polysaccharide joined by a covalent bond.

Liquids

A substance that flows readily in its natural state.

Liver

The bile-secreting organ of an animal, used as food. A dark reddish-brown.

Locomotor

Of or relating to locomotion

Locus

A particular place along the length of a certain chromosome where a given gene is located.

Logistic population growth

A model describing population growth that levels off as population size approaches carrying capacity.

Long-day plant

A plant that flowers, usually in late spring or early summer, only when the light period is longer than a critical length.

Loop of Henle

The long hairpin turn, with a descending and ascending limb, of the renal tubule in the vertebrate kidney; functions in water and salt reabsorption.

Lumen

The cavity of a tubular structure, such as endoplasmic reticulum or a blood vessel.

Lungs

The invaginated respiratory surfaces of terrestrial vertebrates, land snails, and spiders that connect to the atmosphere by narrow tubes.

Leucoplasts

A colourless plastid in the cytoplasm of plant cells that makes and stores starch.

Luteinizing hormone (LH)

A protein hormone secreted by the anterior pituitary that stimulates ovulation in females and androgen production in males.

Lymph

The colourless fluid, derived from interstitial fluid, in the lymphatic system of vertebrate animals.

Lymph node

A mass of spongy tissues, separated into compartments; located throughout the lymphatic system, lymph nodes remove dead cells, debris, and foreign particles from the circulation; also are sites at which foreign antigens are displayed to immunologically active cells.

Lymphatic system

A system of vessels and lymph nodes, separate from the circulatory system, that returns fluid and protein to the blood.

Lymphocyte

A white blood cell. The lymphocytes that complete their development in the bone marrow are called B cells, and those that mature in the thymus are called T cells.

Lymphokine

A chemical, released by an activated cytotoxic T cell, that attracts macrophages and stimulates phagocytosis.

Lysis

The disintegration of a cell by rupture of its plasma membrane.

Lysogenic bacteria

Bacteria carrying a bacteriophage integrated into the bacterial chromosome. The virus may subsequently set up an active cycle of infection, causing lysis of the bacterial cells.

lysogenic cycle

A type of phage replication cycle in which the viral genome becomes incorporated into the bacterial host chromosome as a prophage.

Lysosomes

A membrane-enclosed bag of hydrolytic enzymes found in the cytoplasm of eukaryotic cells.

Lymph vessel

A tubular passage for conveying lymph. Also known as lymphatic.

Lysozyme

An enzyme in perspiration, tears, and saliva that attacks bacterial cell walls.

Lytic cycle

A type of viral replication cycle resulting in the release of new phages by death or lysis of the host cell.

M

M phase

The mitotic phase of the cell cycle, which includes mitosis and cytokinesis.

Macroevolution

Evolutionary change on a grand scale, encompassing the origin of novel designs, evolutionary trends, adaptive radiation, and mass extinction.

Macromolecule

A giant molecule of living matter formed by the joining of smaller molecules, usually by condensation synthesis. Polysaccharides, proteins, and nucleic acids are macromolecules.

Macronutrient

An inorganic nutrient required in large amounts for plant growth, such as nitrogen, potassium, calcium, phosphorus, magnesium, and sulfur.

Macrophage

An amoeboid cell that moves through tissue fibres, engulfing bacteria and dead cells by phagocytosis.

Major histocompatibility complex (MHC)

A large set of cell surface antigens encoded by a family of genes. Foreign MHC markers trigger T-cell responses that may lead to the rejection of transplanted tissues and organs.

Malignant

Dangerous to health; characterized by progressive and uncontrolled growth (especially of a tumour)

Malpighian tubule

A unique excretory organ of insects that empties into the digestive tract, removes nitrogenous wastes from the blood, and functions in osmoregulation.

Mammalia

The vertebrate class of mammals, characterized by body hair and mammary glands that produce milk to nourish the young.

Mammals

Any of various warm-blooded vertebrate animals of the class Mammalia, including humans, characterized by a covering of hair on the skin and, in the female, milk-producing mammary glands for nourishing the young.

Mammary glands

Milk – secreting organ of female mammals.

Mandible

The lower jaw of a vertebrate animal.

Mantle

A heavy fold of tissue in molluscs that drapes over the visceral mass and may secrete a shell.

Marginal

Forming a margin.

Marine

Living in saltwater.

Marsupial

A mammal, such as a koala, kangaroo, or opossum, whose young complete their embryonic development inside a maternal pouch called the marsupium.

Mass number

The sum of the number of protons and neutrons in an atom's nucleus.

Mast cell

A type of noncirculating white blood cell, found in connective tissue, that is the major protagonist in allergic reactions; when an allergen binds to complementary antibodies on the surface of a mast cell, large amounts of histamine are released from the cell.

Matrix

The nonliving component of connective tissue, consisting of a web of fibres embedded inhomogeneous ground substance that may be liquid, jellylike, or solid.

Matter

Anything that takes up space and has mass.

Maturation

The process through which an organism or body structure arrives at a state of complete development. In dentistry, this is the point at which an individual's teeth have reached their full adult form, size, and function.

Maxillary

Of or relating to a jow or jawbone, especially the upper one.

Maxillary teeth

A similar structure in invertebrates, such as one of the pointed denticles or ridges on the exoskeleton of an arthropod or the shell of a mollusc.

Mechanoreceptor

A sensory receptor that detects physical deformations in the body's environment associated with pressure, touch, stretch, motion, and sound.

Medulla

The inner, as opposed to the outer, part of an organ, as in the adrenal gland.

Medulla oblongata

The lowest part of the vertebrate brain; swelling of the hindbrain dorsal to the anterior spinal cord that controls autonomic, homeostatic functions, including breathing, heart and blood vessel activity, swallowing, digestion, and vomiting.

Medullary Rays

Characteristic radial sheets or ribbons extending vertically found in woods

Medusa

The floating, flattened, mouth-down version of the cnidarian body plan. The alternate form is the polyp.

Megabase pairs

One of the pairs of chemical bases joined by hydrogen bonds that connect the complementary strands of a DNA molecule or of an RNA molecule that has two strands; the base pairs are adenine with thymine and guanine with cytosine in DNA and adenine with uracil and guanine with cytosine in RNA

Megapascal (MPa)

A unit of pressure equivalent to 10 atmospheres of pressure.

Megaspore

In plants, a haploid spore that develops into a female gametophyte.

Meiosis or reduction division

A two-stage type of cell division in sexually reproducing organisms that results in gametes with half the chromosome number of the original cell.

Melanoma

A tumour arising from the melanocytic system of the skin and other organs.

Melanocyte -stimulating hormone

A hormone secreted by the pituitary gland that regulates skin colour in humans and other vertebrates by stimulating melanin synthesis in melanocytes and melanin granule dispersal in melanophores. Also called *intermedin*.

Membrane potential

The charge difference between the cytoplasm and extracellular fluid in all cells, due to the differential distribution of ions. Membrane potential affects the activity of excitable cells and the transmembrane movement of all charged substances.

Memory cell

A clone of long-lived lymphocytes, formed during the primary immune response, that remains in a lymph node until activated by exposure to the same antigen that triggered its formation. Activated memory cells mount the secondary immune response.

Mendel's first law

The principle, originated by Gregor Mendel, stating that during the production of gametes the two copies of each hereditary factor segregate so that offspring acquire one factor from each parent.

Mendel's second law

The principle, originated by Gregor Mendel, stating that when two or more characteristics are inherited, individual hereditary factors assort independently during gamete production, giving different traits an equal opportunity of occurring together.

Meniscus

The curved top surface of a column of liquid.

Menstrual cycle

A type of reproductive cycle in higher female primates, in which the nonpregnant endometrium is shed as a bloody discharge through the cervix into the vagina.

Meristem

Plant tissue that remains embryonic as long as the plant lives, allowing for indeterminate growth.

Meristematic cells

A meristem is a tissue in all plants consisting of undifferentiated cells (meristematic cells) and found in zones of the plant where growth can take place.

Meroblastic cleavage

A type of cleavage in which there is an incomplete division of yolk-rich egg, characteristic of avian development.

Mesentery

A membrane that suspends many of the organs of vertebrates inside fluid-filled body cavities.

Mesocarp

The middle, usually fleshy layer of a fruit wall.

Mesoderm

The middle primary germ layer of an early embryo that develops into the notochord, the lining of the coelom, muscles, skeleton, gonads, kidneys, and most of the circulatory system.

Mesoglea

The layer of gelatinous material that separates the inner and outer cell layers of a coelenterate

Mesophyll

The ground tissue of a leaf sandwiched between the upper and lower epidermis and specialized for

Mesonephric

excretory tube of the mesonephros; becomes the mesonephric duct and contributes in the adult to the vasa efferentia of the male.

Mesonephric tubules are genital ridges that are next to the mesonephros. The excretory organ serving as the adult kidney of fishes and amphibians and as the embryonic kidney of higher vertebrates: the mesonephros and its duct develop into the epididymis and vas deferens in higher vertebrates

Mesozoic

Belonging to, or designating the era of geologic time that includes the Triassic, Jurassic, and Cretaceous periods and is characterized by the development of flying reptiles, birds, and flowering plants and by the appearance and extinction of dinosaurs.

Messenger RNA (mRNA)

A type of RNA synthesized from DNA in the genetic material that attaches to ribosomes in the cytoplasm and specifies the primary structure of a protein.

Metabolism

The totality of an organism's chemical processes, consisting of catabolic and anabolic pathways.

Metacarpals

Any bone of the hand between the wrist and fingers

Metacentric

Having the centromere in the median position so that the arms are of equal length. Used of a chromosome.

Metagenesis

Alternation of sexual and asexual generations.

Metamere

Any of the homologous segments, lying in a longitudinal series, that compose the body of certain, such as earthworms and lobsters. Also called *somite.*

Metanephric

One of the three embryonic excretory organs of higher vertebrates, becoming the permanent and functional kidney.

metamorphosis

The resurgence of development in an animal larva that transforms it into a sexually mature adult.

Metanephridim

In annelid worms, a type of excretory tubule with internal openings called nephrostomes that collect body fluids and external openings called nephridiopores.

Metaphase

The second stage of mitosis. During metaphase, all the cell's duplicated chromosomes are lined up at an imaginary plane equidistant between the poles of the mitotic spindle.

Metaphase plate

An imaginary plane perpendicular to the spindle fibres of a dividing cell, along which chromosomes align during metaphase.

Metapopulation

A subdivided population of a single species.

Metastasis

The spread of cancer cells beyond their original site.

MHC

Abbreviation of major histocompatibility complex.

Microbe

A microscopic organism.

Microevolution

A change in the gene pool of a population over a succession of generations.

Microfilaments

A solid rod of actin protein in the cytoplasm of almost all eukaryotic cells, making up a part of the cytoskeleton and acting alone or with myosin to cause cell contraction.

Microglia

Any of the small neuroglial cells of the central nervous system having long processes and amoeboid and phagocytic activity at sites of neural damage or inflammation.

Micronutrient

An inorganic nutrient required in the only minute amounts for plant growth, such as iron, chlorine, copper, manganese, zinc, molybdenum, and boron.

Micropyle

A pore in the membrane covering the ovum of some animals through which a spermatozoon can enter.

Microspore

In plants, a haploid spore that develops into a male gametophyte; in seed plants, it becomes a pollen grain.

Microtubules

A hollow rod of tubulin protein in the cytoplasm of all eukaryotic cells and cilia, flagella, and the cytoskeleton.

Microtubule Organizing Center

The microtubule-organizing centre (MTOC) is a structure found in eukaryotic cells from which microtubules emerge.

Microvillus

One of many fine, fingerlike projections of the epithelial cells in the lumen of the small intestine that increase its surface area.

Middle lamella

A thin layer of adhesive extracellular material, primarily pectins, found between the primary walls of adjacent young plant cells.

Midgut

The middle portion of the digestive tube in vertebrate embryos. Also known as mesenteron.

Mimicry

A phenomenon in which one species benefits by a superficial resemblance to an unrelated species. A predator or species of prey may gain a significant advantage through mimicry.

Mineral

In nutrition, one of many chemical elements, other than carbon, hydrogen, oxygen, and nitrogen, that an organism requires for proper body functioning.

Mineralocorticosteroid

A corticosteroid hormone secreted by the adrenal cortex that regulates salt and water homeostasis.

Minimum dynamic area

The amount of suitable habitat needed to sustain a viable population.

Minimum viable population size (MVP)

The smallest number of individuals needed to perpetuate a population.

missense mutation

The most common type of mutation involving a base-pair substitution within a gene that changes a codon, but the new codon makes sense in that it still codes for an amino acid.

mitochondrial matrix

The compartment of the mitochondrion enclosed by the inner membrane and containing enzymes and substrates for the Krebs cycle.

Mitochondrion

An organelle in eukaryotic cells that serves as the site of cellular respiration.

Mitosis

A process of nuclear division in eukaryotic cells conventionally divided into five stages: prophase, prometaphase, metaphase, anaphase, and telophase. Mitosis conserves chromosome number by equally allocating replicated chromosomes to each of the daughter nuclei.

Modern synthesis

A comprehensive theory of evolution emphasizing natural selection, gradualism, and populations as the fundamental units of evolutionary change; also called neo-Darwinism.

Molars

A large back tooth specialized for crushing and chewing food.

Molarity

A common measure of solute concentration, referring to the number of moles of solute in 1 L of solution.

Mould

A rapidly growing, asexually reproducing fungus.

Mole

The number of grams of a substance that equals its molecular weight in daltons and contains Avogadro's number of molecules.

Molecular formula

A type of molecular notation indicating only the quantity of the constituent atoms.

Molecular weight

The sum of the atomic weights of the constituent atoms in a molecule.

Biologynary

Molecule

Two or more atoms held together by covalent bonds.

Moulting

A process in arthropods in which the exoskeleton is shed at intervals to allow growth by the secretion of a larger exoskeleton.

Monera

In some systems of classification, the kingdom that includes the bacteria, blue-green algae, and other microorganisms with prokaryotic cells.

Monochlamydeous flowers

Having a single floral envelope, that is, a calyx without a corolla, or, possibly, in rare cases, a corolla without a calyx.

Monoclonal antibody

A defensive protein produced by cells descended from a single cell; an antibody that is secreted by a clone of cells and, consequently, is specific for a single antigenic determinant.

Monocot

A subdivision of flowering plants whose members possess one embryonic seed leaf, or cotyledon.

Monocotyledons

A member of the class of flowering plants having one seed leaf, or cotyledon, among other distinguishing features; often abbreviated as a monocot.

Monoculture

Cultivation of large land areas with a single plant variety.

Monoecious

Referring to a plant species that has both staminate and carpellate flowers on the same individual.

Monohybrid

A hybrid individual that is heterozygous for one gene or a single character.

Monohybrid cross

A breeding experiment that uses parental varieties differing in a single character.

Monomer

The subunit that serves as the building block of a polymer.

monophyletic

About a taxon derived from a single ancestral species that gave rise to no species in any other taxa.

Monosaccharide

A The simplest carbohydrate, acting alone or serving as a monomer for disaccharides and polysaccharides. Also known as simple sugars, the molecular formulas of monosaccharides are generally some multiple of CH_2O.

monotreme

An egg-laying mammal, represented by the platypus and echidna.

Monounsaturated

Relating to an organic compound, usually a fatty acid, having only one double bond per molecule.

Morel

An edible mushroom with a pitted cap.

Morphogen

A substance, such as a bicoid protein, that provides positional information in the form of a concentration gradient along an embryonic axis.

Morphogenesis

The development of body shape and organization during ontogeny.

Morphological

About form and structure, at any level of organization.

Morphological species concept

The idea that species are defined by measurable anatomical criteria.

Morphology

The form and structure of an organism and its parts.

Morphospecies

A species defined by its anatomical features.

Mortality rate

Death rate.

Mosaic development

A pattern of development, such as that of a mollusc, in which the early blastomeres each give rise to a specific part of the embryo. In some animals, the fate of the blastomeres is established in the zygote.

Mosaic evolution

The evolution of different features of an organism at different rates.

Motor neuron

A nerve cell that transmits signals from the brain or spinal cord to muscles or glands.

Motor unit

A single motor neuron and all the muscle fibres it controls.

Morula

The spherical embryonic mass of blastomeres formed before the blastula and resulting from cleavage of the fertilized ovum

Moulting

To shed periodically part or all of a coat or an outer covering, such as feathers, cuticle, or skin, which is then replaced by new growth.

MPF (M-phase promoting factor)

A protein complex required for a cell to progress from late interphase to mitosis; the active form consists of cyclin and cdc2, a protein kinase.

Muscle fibre

Muscle cell; a long, cylindrical, multinucleated cell containing numerous myofibrils, which is capable of contraction when stimulated.

M Phase

The entire process of cell division including division of the nucleus and the cytoplasm.

mRNA

RNA, synthesized from a DNA template during transcription, that mediates the transfer of genetic information from the cell nucleus to ribosomes in the cytoplasm, where it serves as a template for protein synthesis. Also called *messenger RNA*.

Mucilage

A gummy substance obtained from certain plants.

Mullerian mimicry

A mutual mimicry by two unpalatable species.

Multicellular

Consisting of many cells

Multigene family

A collection of genes with similar or identical sequences, presumably of common origin.

Musculature

The system or arrangement of muscles in a body or a body part.

Mutagen

A chemical or physical agent that interacts with DNA and causes a mutation.

Mutagenesis

The creation of mutations.

Mutant

An organism carrying a gene that has undergone a mutation.

Mutation

A rare chance in the DNA of genes that ultimately creates genetic diversity.

Mutualism

A symbiotic relationship in which both the host and the symbiont benefit.

Mycelium

The densely branched network of hyphae in a fungus.

Mucilage

A gummy substance obtained from certain plants.

Mycorrhizae

Mutualistic associations of plant roots and fungi.

Myelin sheath

In a neuron, an insulating coat of cell membrane from Schwann cells that are interrupted by nodes of Ranvier where saltatory conduction occurs.

Myofibril

A fibril collectively arranged in longitudinal bundles in muscle cells (fibres); composed of thin filaments of actin and a regulatory protein and thick filaments of myosin.

Myoglobin

An oxygen-storing, pigmented protein in muscle cells.

Myosin

A type of protein filament that interacts with actin filaments to cause cell contraction.

N

NAD⁺ (nicotinamide adenine dinucleotide)

Abbreviation of nicotinamide adenine dinucleotide, a coenzyme present in all cells that helps enzymes transfer electrons during the redox reactions of metabolism.

NADP

Abbreviation of nicotinamide adenine dinucleotide phosphate, a coenzyme that functions as an electron acceptor in the light-dependent reactions of photosynthesis.

Natural killer cell

A nonspecific defensive cell that attacks tumour cells and destroys infected body cells, especially those harbouring viruses.

Natural logarithm

The logarithm to base e where $e \approx 2.718$. The natural logarithm is represented by the symbol ln.

Natural selection

Differential success in the reproduction of different phenotypes resulting from the interaction of organisms with their environment. Evolution occurs when natural selection causes changes in relative frequencies of alleles in the gene pool.

Nectar

A sugary fluid that attracts insects to plants.

Negative feedback

A primary mechanism of homeostasis, whereby a change in a physiological variable that is being monitored triggers a response that counteracts the initial fluctuation.

Nematocyst

A threadlike stinger, containing a poisonous or paralyzing substance, found in the cnidocyte of cnidarians.

Nemertea

An equivalent name for Rhynchocoela.

Nephridium

A tubular excretory structure found in many invertebrates.

Nephrons

The tubular excretory unit of the vertebrate kidney.

Neritic zone

The shallow regions of the ocean overlying the continental shelves.

Nerve

A rope-like bundle of neuron fibres (axons and dendrites) tightly wrapped in connective tissue.

Nervechord

Nerve chord is also called a spinal cord; a hollow structure that extends the length of the animal just above the notochord.

Nerve fibre

A filamentous process extending from the cell body of a neuron and conducting the nerve impulse; an axon.

Nerve impulse

A rapid, transient, self-propagating change in electric potential across the membrane of an axon.

Nervous system

All the nerve cells of an animal; the receptor-conductor-effector system; in humans, the nervous system consists of the central nervous system (brain and spinal cord) and the peripheral nervous system.

Net primary production

In a community or an ecosystem, the increase in the amount of plant or algal material between the beginning and end of a specified period, such as a growing season.

Net primary productivity(NPP)

The gross primary productivity minus the energy used by the producers for cellular respiration; represents the storage of chemical energy in an ecosystem available to consumers.

Net productivity

In a trophic level, a community, or an ecosystem, the amount of energy (in calories) stored in chemical compounds or the increase in biomass (in grams or metric tons) in a particular period; it is the difference between gross productivity and the energy used by the organisms in respiration.

Neural crest

A band of cells along the border where the neural tube pinches off from the ectoderm; the cells migrate to various parts of the embryo and form the pigment cells in the skin, bones of the skull, the teeth, the adrenal glands, and parts of the peripheral nervous system.

Neural groove

Dorsal, longitudinal groove that forms in a vertebrate embryo; bordered by two neural folds; preceded by the neural-plate stage and followed by the neural-tube stage.

Neural plate

A thickened strip of ectoderm in early vertebrate embryos that form along the dorsal side of the body and gives rise to the central nervous system.

Neural tube

The primitive, hollow, dorsal nervous system of the early vertebrate embryo; formed by the fusion of neural folds around the neural groove.

Neuromodulator

A chemical agent that is released by a neuron and diffuses through a local region of the central nervous system, acting on neurons within that region; generally has the effect of modulating the response to neurotransmitters.

Neuromuscular junction

The junction between an axon terminal of a motor neuron and a muscle fibre innervated by that motor neuron; the axon terminal of a motor neuron is typically branched, forming neuromuscular junctions with some different muscle fibres.

Neuron

A nerve cell; the fundamental unit of the nervous system, having structure and properties that allow it to conduct signals by taking advantage of the electrical charge across its cell membrane.

Neurosecretory cells

Hypothalamus cells that receive signals from other nerve cells, but instead of signalling to an adjacent nerve cell or muscle, they release hormones into the bloodstream.

Neurotransmitter

A chemical messenger released from the synaptic terminal of a neuron at a chemical synapse that diffuses across the synaptic cleft and binds to and stimulates the postsynaptic cell.

Neutral variation

Genetic diversity that confers no apparent selective advantage.

Neutron

An electrically neutral particle (a particle having no electrical charge), found in the atom.

Niche

The position or function of an organism in a community of plants and animals.

Nematocyst

A capsule within specialized cells of certain coelenterates, such as jellyfish, containing a barbed, threadlike tube that delivers a paralyzing sting when propelled into attackers and prey. *Also called a stinging cell.*

Nictitating membrane

A protective fold of skin in the eyes of reptiles and birds and some mammals

Nitrification

The oxidation of ammonia or ammonium to nitrites and nitrates, as by nitrifying bacteria.

Nitrogen cycle

Worldwide circulation and reutilization of nitrogen atoms, chiefly due to metabolic processes of living organisms; plants take up inorganic nitrogen and convert it into organic compounds (chiefly proteins), which are assimilated into the bodies of one or more animals; bacterial and fungal action on nitrogenous waste products and dead organisms return nitrogen atoms to the inorganic state.

Nitrogen fixation

The assimilation of atmospheric nitrogen by certain prokaryotes into nitrogenous compounds that can be directly used by plants.

Nitrogenase

An enzyme, unique to certain prokaryotes, that reduces N_2 to NH_3.

Nitrogenous base

An organic base that contains the element nitrogen.

Nitrogenous compounds

Nitrogen a chemical element, at no.7. it forms about 78 per cent of the atmosphere and is a constituent of all proteins and nucleic acids.

Nocturnal

Applied to organisms that are active during the hours of darkness.

Node

A point along the stem of a plant at which leaves are attached.

Nodes of Ranvier

The small gaps in the myelin sheath between successive glial cells along the axon of a neuron; also, the site of high concentration of voltage-gated ion channels.

Nomograph

A graph that allows a third variable to be measured when the values of two related variables are known.

Noncompetitive inhibitor

A substance that reduces the activity of an enzyme by binding to a location remote from the active site, changing its conformation so that it no longer binds to the substrate.

Noncyclic electron flow

A route of electron flow during the light reactions of photosynthesis that involves both photosystems and produces ATP, NADPH, and oxygen; the net electron flow is from water to $NADP^+$.

Noncyclic photophosphorylation

The production of ATP by noncyclic electron flow.

Nondisjunction

An accident of meiosis or mitosis, in which both members of a pair of homologous chromosomes or both sister chromatids fail to move apart properly.

Nonpolar covalent bond

A type of covalent bond in which electrons are shared equally between two atoms of similar electronegativity.

Nonprotoplasmic

The complex, semifluid, translucent substance that constitutes the living matter of plant and animal cells and manifests the essential life functions of a cell. Composed of proteins, fats, and other molecules suspended in water, it includes the nucleus and cytoplasm.

Nonsense mutation

A mutation that changes an amino acid codon to one of the three stop codons, resulting in a shorter and usually nonfunctional protein.

non-sister chromatids

chromatid from two different homolog chromosomes.

Noradrenaline

A hormone, produced by the medulla of the adrenal gland, that increases the concentration of glucose in the blood, raises blood pressure and heartbeat rate, and increases muscular power and resistance to fatigue; also one of the principal neurotransmitters; also called norepinephrine.

Norepinephrine

A substance, $C_8H_{11}NO_3$, both a hormone and neurotransmitter, secreted by the adrenal medulla and the nerve endings of the sympathetic nervous system to cause vasoconstriction and increases in heart rate, blood pressure and the sugar level of the blood. Also called *noradrenaline*.

Norm of reaction

The range of phenotypic possibilities for a single genotype, as influenced by the environment.

Nostril

Either f the external opening of the nose.

Notochord

A longitudinal, flexible rod formed from dorsal mesoderm and located between the gut and the nerve cord in all chordate embryos.

Nuclear envelope

The membrane in eukaryotes that encloses the nucleus, separating it from the cytoplasm.

Nucleic acid

A polymer consisting of many nucleotide monomers; serves as a blueprint for proteins and, through the actions of proteins, for all cellular activities. The two types are DNA and RNA. Nuclear

The scientific study of the forces, reactions, and internal structures of atomic nuclei.

Nuclear envelope

The double-layered membrane enclosing the nucleus of a cell. Also called the *nuclear envelope*.

Nuclear lamina

A protein meshwork lining the inner surface of the nuclear envelope

Nuclear membrane

The double-layered membrane enclosing the nucleus of a cell. Also called the *nuclear envelope*

Nuclear pores

The nuclear envelope is composed of two membranes joined at regular intervals to form circular openings called nuclear pores.

Nucleic acid probe

In DNA technology, a labelled single-stranded nucleic acid molecule used to tag a specific nucleotide sequence in a nucleic acid sample. Molecules of the probe hydrogen-bond to the complementary sequence wherever it occurs; radioactive or another labelling of the probe allows its location to be detected.

Nucleoid

A dense region of DNA in a prokaryotic cell.

Nucleoid region

The region in a prokaryotic cell consisting of a concentrated mass of DNA.

Nucleolus

A specialized structure in the nucleus, formed from various chromosomes and active in the synthesis of ribosomes.

Nuclear sap/nucleoplasm

Similar to the cytoplasm of a cell, the nucleus contains nuclear sap or nucleoplasm. The nucleoplasm is one of the types of protoplasm, and it is enveloped by the nuclear membrane or nuclear envelope.

Nucleoproteins

Any of a group of complexes composed of protein and nucleic acid and found in the nuclei and cytoplasm of all living cells, as in chromatin and ribosomes.

Nucleoplasm

The protoplasm that constitutes the nucleus of a cell. Or The jellylike material within a cell nucleus, containing the nucleolus and chromatin.

Nucleoside

An organic molecule consisting of a nitrogenous base joined to a five-carbon sugar.

Nucleosome

The basic, beadlike unit of DNA packaging in eukaryotes, consisting of a segment of DNA wound around a protein core composed of two copies of each of four types of histone.

Nucleotide

The building block of nucleic acid, consisting of a five-carbon sugar covalently bonded to a nitrogenous base and a phosphate group.

Nucleus

(1)   An atom's central core, containing protons and neutrons.

(2)   The chromosome-containing organelle of a eukaryotic cell.

Null hypothesis

In statistical analysis, a hypothesis proposing that there is no statistically significant difference between the observed results of an experiment and the expected results. **Neurotransmitter metabolism**

Sum of chemical changes that occur within the tissues of an organism consisting of anabolism (biosynthesis) and catabolism of neurotransmitters; the buildup and breakdown of neurotransmitters for utilization by the organism.

O

Obligate aerobe

An organism that requires oxygen for cellular respiration and cannot live without it.

Obligate anaerobe

An organism that cannot use oxygen and is poisoned by it.

Occipital condyle

An articular surface on the occipital bone which articulates with the atlas. (invertebrate zoology) A projection on the posterior border of an insect head which articulates with the lateral neck plates.

Oceanic zone

The region of water lying over deep areas beyond the continental shelf.

Ocelli

Simple eyes of insects.

Offset

A short runner in certain plants that produce roots and shoots at the tip.

Oils

Flammable substance, usually insoluble in water, and composed chiefly of carbon and hydrogen. Oils may be solids (fats and waxes) or liquids. Various plants produce vegetable oils; mineral oils are based on petroleum.

Oligodendrocytes

One of the cells comprising the oligodendroglia.

Oligosaccharides

A carbohydrate that consists of a relatively small number of monosaccharides.

Oligotrophic lake

A nutrient-poor, clear, deep lake with minimum phytoplankton.

Omnivore

A heterotrophic animal that consumes both meat and plant material.

Oncogenes

A gene found in viruses or as part of the normal genome that is involved in triggering cancerous characteristics.

Ontogeny

The embryonic development of an organism.

Oocyte

A cell that gives rise by meiosis to an ovum.

Oogamy

A condition in which male and female gametes differ, such that a small, flagellated sperm fertilizes a large, nonmotile egg.

Oogenesis

The process in the ovary that results in the production of female gametes.

Open circulatory system

An arrangement of internal transport in which blood bathes the organs directly and there is no distinction between blood and interstitial fluid.

Operant conditioning

A type of associative learning that directly affects behaviour in a natural context; also called trial-and-error learning.

Operator

A segment of DNA that interacts with a repressor protein to regulate the transcription of the structural genes of an operon.

Operculum

A covering flap or lidlike structure in animals like snails, some fishes.

Operon

A unit of genetic function common in bacteria and phages, consisting of coordinately regulated clusters of genes with related functions.

Opportunistic species

Species characterized by high reproduction rates, rapid development, early reproduction, small body size, and uncertain adult survival.

Opsonization

An immune response in which the binding of antibodies to the surface of a microbe facilitates phagocytosis of the microbe by a macrophage.

Oral

Of or relating to the mouth.

Orbital

In the current model of atomic structure, the volume of space surrounding the atomic nucleus in which an electron will be found 90 per cent of the time.

Order

A taxonomic grouping of related, similar families; the category below class and above family.

Organ

A specialized centre of body function composed of several different types of tissues.

Organ-identity gene

A plant gene in which a mutation causes a floral organ to develop in the wrong location.

Organ level

A disturbance involving the transport or metabolic functions of an organ.

Organ of Corti

The actual hearing organ of the vertebrate ear, located in the floor of the cochlear canal in the inner ear; contains the receptor cells (hair cells) of the ear.

Organelle

One of several formed bodies with a specialized function, suspended in the cytoplasm and found in eukaryotic cells.

Organic

(1)   organisms or living things generally

(2)   compounds formed by living organisms

3) the chemistry of compounds containing carbon.

Organ system

A group of related organs is an organ system

Organic chemistry

The study of carbon compounds (organic compounds).

Organic compound

A chemical compound containing the element carbon and usually synthesized by cells.

Organism

An individual living thing, such as a bacterium, fungus, protist, plant or animal.

Organogenesis

An early period of rapid embryonic development in which the organs take form from the primary germ layers.

Orgasm

Rhythmic, involuntary contractions of certain reproductive structures in both sexes during the human sexual response cycle.

Origin of replication

A specific sequence of bases in a nucleic acid molecule to which the enzymes responsible for replicating the nucleic acid bind to initiate the copying process.

Orthotropous

Completely straight with the micropyle at the apex.

Osculum

The mouth-like opening in a sponge used to expel water.

Osmoconformer

An animal that does not actively adjust its internal osmolarity because it is isotonic with its environment.

Osmolarity

Solute concentration expressed as molarity.

Osmoregulation

Adaptations to control the water balance in organisms living in hypertonic, hypotonic, or terrestrial environments.

Osmoregulator

An animal whose body fluids have a different osmolarity than the environment and that must either discharge excess water if it lives in a hypotonic environment or takes in water if it inhabits a hypertonic environment.

Osmosis

The diffusion of water across a selectively permeable membrane.

Osmotic potential

The tendency of water to move across a selectively permeable membrane into a solution; it is determined by measuring the pressure required to stop the osmotic movement of water into the solution.

Osmotic pressure

A measure of the tendency of a solution to take up water when separated from pure water by a selectively permeable membrane.

Ossicle

A small bone, especially one of the three bones of the middle ear.

Osphradium

The olfactory organ of some Mollusca. It is connected with the organ of respiration.

Osteichthyes

The vertebrate class of bony fishes, characterized by a skeleton reinforced by calcium phosphate; the most abundant and diverse vertebrates.

Ostia

The water moves into the spongocoel in Porifera through Ostia

Ostracoderm

An extinct agnathan; a fishlike creature encased in an armour of bony plates.

Outgroup

A species or group of species that is closely related to the group of species being studied, but not as closely related as any study-group members are to each other.

Ovaries

The usually paired female or hermaphroditic reproductive organ that produces ova and, in vertebrates, estrogen and progesterone.

Ovarian cycle

The cyclic recurrence of the follicular phase, ovulation, and the luteal phase in the mammalian ovary, regulated by hormones.

Ovarian follicle

A developing oocyte and the specialized cells surrounding it; located near the surface of the ovary; following ovulation, forms the corpus luteum.

Ovary

1) In flowers, the portion of a carpel in which the egg-containing ovules develop.

(2) In animals, the structure that produces female gametes and reproductive hormones.

Oviduct

A tube passing from the ovary to the vagina in invertebrates or to the uterus in vertebrates.

Oviparous

Referring to a type of development in which young hatch from eggs laid outside the mother's body.

Ovoviviparous

Referring to a type of development in which young hatch from eggs that are retained in the mother's uterus.

Ovulation

The release of an egg from ovaries. In humans, an ovarian follicle releases an egg during each menstrual cycle.

Ovule

A structure that develops in the plant ovary and contains the female gametophyte.

Ovum

The female gamete; the haploid, unfertilized egg, which is usually a relatively large, nonmotile cell.

Oxidation

The loss of electrons from a substance involved in a redox reaction.

Oxidative phosphorylation

The production of ATP using energy derived from the redox reactions of an electron transport chain.

Oxidizing agent

The electron acceptor in a redox reaction.

Oxygen debt

In muscle, the cumulative deficit of oxygen that develops during strenuous exercise when the supply of oxygen is inadequate for the demand; ATP is produced anaerobically by glycolysis, and the resulting pyruvic acid is converted to lactic acid, which is subsequently metabolized when adequate oxygen is available.

Oxysomes/F1 particles.

Oxysomes are also called elementary particles or F_1 particles. They are helpful in the electron transport of respiration that is in oxidation and reduction reactions.

P

Pacemaker

A specialized region of the right atrium of the mammalian heart that sets the rate of contraction; also called the sinoatrial (SA) node.

Pachytene

The third stage of the prophase of meiosis during which the homologous chromosomes become short and thick and divide into four distinct chromatids.

Paedogenesis

The precocious development of sexual maturity in a larva.

Paedomorphosis

The retention in an adult organism of the juvenile features of its evolutionary ancestors.

Palaeontology

The scientific study of fossils.

Polysaccharides

A carbohydrate which consists of several linked sugar molecules, such as starch or cellulose.

Palisade cells

In-plant leaves, the columnar, chloroplast-containing parenchyma cells of the mesophyll.

Palisade parenchyma

A leaf tissue composed of columnar cells containing numerous chloroplasts in which the long axis of each cell is perpendicular to the leaf surface.

Pallium

A protective layer of the epidermis in molluscs or brachiopods that secretes a substance forming the shell.

Palisade parenchyma

A leaf tissue composed of columnar cells containing numerous chloroplasts in which the long axis of each cell is perpendicular to the leaf surface.

Pancreas

In vertebrates, a small, complex gland located between the stomach and the duodenum, which produces digestive enzymes and the hormones insulin and glucagon.

Pangaea

The supercontinent formed near the end of the Paleozoic era when plate movements brought all the landmasses of Earth together.

Paramecium

Any of various freshwater ciliate protozoans of the genus *Paramecium,* usually oval and having an oral groove for feeding.

Paramylum

A carbohydrate resembling starch that is composed of glucose and forms the reserve foodstuff of certain algae.

Paraphyletic

About a taxon that excludes some members that share a common ancestor with members included in the taxon.

Parapodia

One of a pair of fleshy appendages of a polychaete annelid that functions in locomotion and breathing.

Parasite

An organism that absorbs nutrients from the body fluids of living hosts.

Parasitic

Relating to or caused by parasites; "parasitic infection"

Parasitism

A symbiotic relationship in which the symbiont (parasite) benefits at the expense of the host by living either within the host (endoparasite) or outside the host (ectoparasite).

Parasympathetic division

One of two divisions of the autonomic nervous system; generally enhances body activities that gain and conserve energy, such as digestion and reduced heart rate.

Parathyroid glands

Four endocrine glands, embedded in the surface of the thyroid gland, that secrete parathyroid hormone and raise blood calcium levels.

Parazoa

Members of the subkingdom of animals consisting of the sponges.

Parenchyma

A relatively unspecialized plant cell type that carries most of the metabolism, synthesizes and stores organic products, and develops into more differentiated cell types.

Parental generation

In an experimental genetic cross, the parents of the F1 generation; homozygous for the trait(s) being studied.

Parietal

Borne on the inside of the ovary wall. Used of the ovules or placentas in flowering plants.

Parthenogenesis

A type of reproduction in which females produce offspring from unfertilized eggs.

Particle

A very small piece or part; a tiny portion or speck.

Parietal

Relating to or forming the wall of a body part, organ, or cavity.

Partial pressures

The concentration of gases; a fraction of total pressure.

Passive transport

The diffusion of a substance across a biological membrane.

Pathogen

An organism or a virus that causes disease.

Parthenocarpic

The production of fruit without fertilization.

Pattern formation

The ordering of cells into specific three-dimensional structures, an essential part of shaping an organism and its parts during development.

Pericardium

He membranous sac filled with serous fluid that encloses the heart and the roots of the aorta and other large blood vessels

Pectin

Pectin is a gummy polysaccharide constituent of the cell walls of plants that are used as a thickening agent in jams and jellies. Pectin's mucilaginous qualities are useful in treating diarrhoea and high cholesterol and it may have beneficial effects on radiation sickness as well.

Pedigree

A family tree describing the occurrence of heritable characters in parents and offspring across as many generations as possible.

Pelagic zone

The area of the ocean past the continental shelf, with areas of open water often reaching to very great depths.

Pelvic girdle

A bony or cartilaginous structure in vertebrates, attached to and supporting the hind limbs or fins.

Penis

The male organ of copulation in higher vertebrates, homologous with the clitoris (female). In mammals, it also serves as the male organ of urinary excretion.

Pentadactyl

Having five fingers or toes on each hand or foot.

Pentose

Any of a class of simple sugars having five carbon atoms per molecule. Ribose and deoxyribose are pentoses.

Penetrance

In genetics, the proportion of individuals with a particular genotype that shows the phenotype ascribed to that genotype.

Peptide bond

The covalent bond between two amino acid units, formed by condensation synthesis.

Peptidyl transferase

A ribosome-associated protein that has the peptidyl transferase activity needed to synthesize peptide bonds during translation has never been isolated. The reason for this lack of success is now known: the enzyme activity is specified by part of the 23S rRNA.

Peptidoglycan

A type of polymer in bacterial cell walls consisting of modified sugars cross-linked by short polypeptides.

Perception

The interpretation of sensations by the brain.

Perennial

A plant that lives for many years.

Pericycle

A layer of cells just inside the endodermis of a root that may become meristematic and begin dividing again.

Periderm

The protective coat that replaces the epidermis in plants during secondary growth, formed of the cork and cork cambium.

Pericardial

The membranous sac filled with serous fluid that encloses the heart and the roots of the aorta and other large blood vessels.

Perigynous

Having sepals, petals, and stamens around the edge of a cuplike receptacle containing the ovary, as in flowers of the rose or cherry.

Peripheral nervous system

The sensory and motor neurons that connect to the central nervous system.

Peristalsis

Rhythmic waves of contraction of smooth muscle that push food along the digestive tract.

Peritoneum

A membrane that lines the body cavity and forms the external covering of the visceral organs.

Peritubular capillaries

In the vertebrate kidney, the capillaries that surround the renal tubule; water and solutes are reabsorbed into the bloodstream through the peritubular capillaries and some substances are secreted from them into the renal tubule.

Permeable

Penetrable by molecules, ions, or atoms; usually applied to membranes that let given solutes pass through.

Peroxisomes

A microbody containing enzymes that transfer hydrogen from various substrates to oxygen, producing and then degrading hydrogen peroxide.

Petiole

The stalk of a leaf, which joins the leaf to a node of the stem.

pH scale

A measure of hydrogen ion concentration equal to $-\log [H^+]$ and ranging in value from 0 to 14.

Phage

A virus that infects bacteria; also called a bacteriophage.

Phagocytosis

A type of endocytosis involving large, particulate substances.

Pharynx

An area in the vertebrate throat where air and food passages cross; in flatworms, the muscular tube that protrudes from the ventral side of the worm and ends in the mouth.

Phenetics

An approach to taxonomy based entirely on measurable similarities and differences in phenotypic characters, without consideration of homology, analogy, or phylogeny.

Phenotype

The physical and physiological traits of an organism.

Pheromone

A small, volatile chemical signal that functions in communication between animals and acts much like a hormone in influencing physiology and behaviour.

Phloem

The portion of the vascular system in plants consisting of living cells arranged into elongated tubes that transport sugar and other organic nutrients throughout the plant.

Phosphate group

A functional group important in energy transfer.

Phospholipids

Molecules that constitute the inner bilayer of biological membranes, having a polar, hydrophilic head and a nonpolar, hydrophobic tail.

Phosphorylation

Addition of a phosphate group or groups to a molecule.

Phosphoester bonds

A phosphodiester bond is a group of strong covalent bonds between the phosphorous atom in a phosphate group and two other molecules over two ester bonds.

Phospholytic

The organic compounds of phosphorus. The blood phosphate level is normally 2.5 mg to 5 mg/100 mL. It is low in rickets and early hyperparathyroidism and high in tetany and nephritis

Photic zone

The narrow top slice of the ocean, where light permeates sufficiently for photosynthesis to occur.

Photoautotroph

An organism that harnesses light energy to drive the synthesis of organic compounds from carbon dioxide.

Photoheterotroph

An organism that uses light to generate ATP but that must obtain carbon in organic form.

Photon

A quantum, or discrete amount, of light energy.

Photoperiodism

Physiological response to day length, such as flowering in plants.

Photophosphorylation

The process of generating ATP from ADP and phosphate using a proton-motive force generated by the thylakoid membrane of the chloroplast during the light reactions of photosynthesis.

Photoreceptor

A cell or organ capable of detecting light.

Photorespiration

A metabolic pathway that consumes oxygen, releases carbon dioxide, generates no ATP, and decreases photosynthetic output; generally occurs on hot, dry, bright days, when stomata close and the oxygen concentration in the leaf exceeds that of carbon dioxide.

Photosynthesis

The conversion of light energy to chemical energy that is stored in glucose or other organic compounds; occurs in plants, algae, and certain prokaryotes.

Photosystem

The light-harvesting unit in photosynthesis, located on the thylakoid membrane of the chloroplast and consisting of the antenna complex, the reaction-centre chlorophyll a, and the primary electron acceptor. There are two types of photosystems, I and II; they absorb light best at different wavelengths.

Phototropism

Growth of a plant shoot toward or away from light.

Phyletic change

The changes taking place in a single lineage of organisms over a long period; one of the principal patterns of evolutionary change.

Phylogeny

The evolutionary history of a species or group of related species.

Phylum, phyla(*Plus*)

A taxonomic category; phyla are divided into classes.

Physiology

The study of function in cells, organs, or entire organisms; the processes of life.

Phytoalexin

An antibiotic, produced by plants, that destroy microorganisms or inhibits their growth.

Phytochrome

A pigment involved in many responses of plants to light.

Phytoplankton

Aquatic, free-floating, microscopic, photosynthetic organisms.

Piercing

Painful as if caused by a sharp instrument

Pigments

A coloured substance that absorbs light over a narrow band of wavelengths.

Pilus

A surface appendage in certain bacteria that functions in adherence and the transfer of DNA during conjugation.

Piliferous layer

The part of the root epidermis that bears root hairs. It extends over a region

Pineal gland

A small endocrine gland on the dorsal surface of the vertebrate forebrain; secretes the hormone melatonin, which regulates body functions related to seasonal day length.

Pinocytosis

A type of endocytosis in which the cell ingests extracellular fluid and its dissolved solutes.

Pith

The core of the central vascular cylinder of monocot roots, consisting of parenchyma cells, which are ringed by vascular tissue; ground tissue interior to vascular bundles in dicot stems.

Pituitary gland

An endocrine gland at the base of the hypothalamus; consists of a posterior lobe (neurohypophysis), which stores and releases two hormones produced by the hypothalamus, and an anterior lobe (adenohypophysis), which produces and secretes many hormones that regulate diverse body functions.

Placenta

A structure in the pregnant uterus for nourishing a viviparous fetus with the mother's blood supply; formed from the uterine lining and embryonic membranes.

Placental mammal

A member of a group of mammals, including humans, whose young complete their embryonic development in the uterus, joined to the mother by a placenta.

Placoderm

A member of an extinct class of fishlike vertebrates that had jaws and were enclosed in a tough, outer armour.

Placoid

As the hard flattened scales of e.g. sharks

Planarians

Any of various small, chiefly freshwater turbellarian flatworms of the order Tricladida, having soft, broad, ciliated bodies, a three-branched digestive cavity, and the ability to regenerate body parts.

Plankton

Mostly microscopic organisms that drift passively or swim weakly near the surface of oceans, ponds, and lakes.

Planula

The ciliated, free-swimming type of larva formed by many cnidarians.

Plasma

The liquid matrix of blood in which the cells are suspended.

Plasma cell

A derivative of B cells that secretes antibodies.

Plasma membrane

The membrane at the boundary of every cell that acts as a selective barrier, thereby regulating the cell's chemical composition.

Plasmid

A small ring of DNA that carries accessory genes separate from those of a bacterial chromosome. Also found in some eukaryotes, such as yeast.

Plasmodesma, plasmodesmata(*Plu*)

An open channel in the cell wall of plants through which strands of cytosol connect from adjacent cells.

Plantae

Plants are a major group of life forms and include familiar organisms such as trees, herbs, bushes, grasses, vines, ferns, mosses, and green algae.

Plasmogamy

The fusion of the cytoplasm of cells from two individuals; occurs as one stage of syngamy.

Plasmolysis

A phenomenon in walled cells in which the cytoplasm shrivels and the plasma membrane pulls away from the cell wall when the cell loses water to a hypertonic environment.

Plasmosome/plasmasome

The true nucleolus of a cell as distinguished from the karyosomes in the nucleus. Also spelt plasma some.

Plastids

One of a family of closely related plant organelles, including chloroplasts, chromoplasts, and amyloplasts.

Platelet

A small enucleated blood cell important in blood clotting; derived from large cells in the bone marrow.

Platyhelminthes

A phylum of invertebrates composed of bilaterally symmetrical, nonsegmented, dorsoventrally flattened worms characterized by lack of coelom, anus, circulatory and respiratory systems, and skeleton.

Pleated sheet

One form of the secondary structure of proteins in which the polypeptide chain folds back and forth, or where two regions of the chain lie parallel to each other and are held together by hydrogen bonds.

Pleiotropy

The ability of a single gene to have multiple effects.

Plesiomorphic character

A primitive phenotypic character possessed by a remote ancestor.

Pluripotent stem cell

A cell within the bone marrow that is a progenitor for any kind of blood cell.

Pneumatic

Having cavities filled with air, as the bones of certain birds.

Pneumatophores

A specialized respiratory root structure in certain aquatic plants, such as the bald cypress.

Poikilotherm

An organism, such as a fish or reptile, having a body temperature that varies with the temperature of its surroundings; an ectotherm.

Point mutation

A change in a gene at a single nucleotide pair.

Polar

Having parts or areas with opposed or contrasting properties, such as positive and negative charges, head and tail.

Polar body

Minute, the nonfunctioning cell produced during those meiotic divisions that lead to egg cells; contains a nucleus but very little cytoplasm.

Polar covalent bond

A type of covalent bond between atoms that differ in electronegativity. The shared electrons are pulled closer to the more electronegative atom, making it slightly negative and the other atom slightly positive.

Polar molecule

A molecule with opposite charges on opposite sides.

Polar nuclei

In angiosperms, the two nuclei of the central cell of the female gametophyte; they fuse with a sperm nucleus to form the triploid ($3n$) endosperm nucleus.

Pollen

An immature male gametophyte that develops within the anthers of stamens in a flower.

Pollination

The placement of pollen onto the stigma of a carpel by wind or animal carriers, a prerequisite to fertilization.

Polyadelphous

United by the filaments into three or more sets or bundles.

Polyandry

A polygamous mating system involving one female and many males.

Polyandrous

Relating to an angiosperm plant that has an indefinite number of stamens in its flowers.

Polyembryony

Development of more than one embryo from a single egg or ovule.

Polygenic inheritance

An additive effect of two or more gene loci on a single phenotypic character.

Polygyny

A polygamous mating system involving one male and many females.

Polymer

A large molecule consisting of many identical or similar monomers linked together.

Polymerase

An enzyme, such as DNA polymerase or RNA polymerase, that catalyzes the synthesis of a polymer from its subunits.

Polymerase chain reaction (PCR)

A technique for amplifying DNA in vitro by incubating with special primers, DNA polymerase molecules and nucleotides.

Polymorphic

Referring to a population in which two or more physical forms are present in readily noticeable frequencies.

Polymorphism

The coexistence of two or more distinct forms of individuals (polymorphic characters) in the same population.

Polynucleotide

A polymer made up of many nucleotides covalently bonded together.

Polyp

The sessile variant of the cnidarian body plan. The alternate form is the medusa.

Polypeptide

A polymer (chain) of many amino acids linked together by peptide bonds.

Polyphyletic

About a taxon whose members were derived from two or more ancestral forms not common to all members.

Polyploid

Cell with more than two complete sets of chromosomes per nucleus.

Polyploidy

A chromosomal alteration in which the organism possesses more than two complete chromosome sets.

Polyribosome

An aggregation of several ribosomes attached to one messenger RNA molecule.

Polysaccharide

A polymer of up to over a thousand monosaccharides, formed by condensation synthesis.

Polysomes

A cluster of ribosomes connected by a strand of messenger RNA and actively synthesizing protein. Also called a *polysome.*

Polyunsaturated fats

Relating to an organic compound, especially a fat, in which more than one pair of carbon atoms are joined by double or triple bonds

Pores

A minute opening in tissue, as in the skin of an animal, serving as an outlet for perspiration, or in a plant leaf or stem, serving as a means of absorption and transpiration.

Population

A group of individuals of one species that live in a particular geographic area.

Population bottleneck

Type of genetic drift that occurs as the result of a population being drastically reduced in numbers by an event having little to do with the usual forces of natural selection.

Population density

The number of individuals of a population per unit area or volume of living space.

Population viability analysis (PVA)

A method of predicting whether or not a species will persist in a particular environment.

Positional information

Signals, to which genes regulating development respond, indicating a cell's location relative to other cells in an embryonic structure.

Positive feedback

A physiological control mechanism in which a change in some variable triggers mechanisms that amplify the change.

Posterior

Of or about the rear end of the body, or tail end.

Postsynaptic membrane

The surface of the cell on the opposite side of the synapse from the synaptic terminal of the stimulating neuron that contains receptor proteins and degradative enzymes for the neurotransmitter.

Postzygotic barrier

Any of several species-isolating mechanisms that prevent hybrids produced by two different species from developing into viable, fertile adults.

Potential energy

The energy stored by matter as a result of its location or spatial arrangement.

Predation

An interaction between species in which one species, the predator, eats the other, the prey.

Predator

An organism that eats other living organisms.

Premolar

A tooth having two cusps or points; located between the incisors and the molars.

Pressure-flow hypothesis

A hypothesis accounting for sap flow through the phloem system. According to this hypothesis, the solution containing nutrient sugars moves through the sieve tubes by bulk flow, moving into and out of the sieve tubes by active transport and diffusion.

Prey

An organism is eaten by another organism.

Prezygotic barrier

A reproductive barrier that impedes mating between species or hinders fertilization of ova if interspecific mating is attempted.

Primary cell walls

A cell wall is a fairly rigid layer surrounding a cell, located external to the cell membrane, which provides the cell with structural support, protection, and acts as a filtering mechanism.

Primary consumer

A herbivore; an organism in the trophic level of an ecosystem that eats plants or algae.

Primary germ layers

The three layers (ectoderm, mesoderm, endoderm) of the late gastrula, which develop into all parts of an animal.

Primary growth

Growth initiated by the apical meristems of a plant root or shoot.

Primary immune response

The initial immune response to an antigen, which appears after a lag of several days.

Primary meristems

Meristematic tissue in vascular plants that are derived from an apical meristem, such as the procambium, protoderm, and ground meristem.

Primary pit fields

The parenchyma cell in the very centre (arrow) appears to be filled with a weblike mesh, but in fact, we are looking at either the front or the back wall, and virtually the entire wall is a set of primary pit fields.

Primary producer

An autotroph, which collectively makes up the trophic level of an ecosystem that ultimately supports all other levels; usually a photosynthetic organism.

Primary productivity

The rate at which light energy or inorganic chemical energy is converted to the chemical energy of organic compounds by autotrophs in an ecosystem.

Primary structure

The level of protein structure refers to the specific sequence of amino acids.

Primary succession

A type of ecological succession that occurs in an area where there were originally no organisms.

Primer

An already existing short RNA chain bound to template DNA to which DNA nucleotides are added during DNA synthesis.

Primate

A member of the order of mammals that includes anthropoids and prosimians.

Primitive

Not specialized; at an early stage of evolution or development.

Primitive streak

A dense, opaque band of ectoderm in the bilaminar blastoderm associated with the morphogenetic movements and proliferation of the mesoderm and notochord; indicates the first trace of the vertebrate embryo.

Primordium

A cell or organ in its earliest stage of differentiation.

Principle of allocation

The concept that each organism has an energy budget or a limited amount of total energy available for all of its maintenance and reproductive needs.

Prion

An infectious form of protein that may increase in number by converting related proteins to more prions.

Probe

Any identifiable substance that is used to detect, isolate, or identify another substance, as a labelled strand of DNA that hybridizes with its complementary RNA or a monoclonal antibody that combines with a specific protein.

Proboscis

A long flexible snout or trunk, as of an elephant.

Procambium

A primary meristem of roots and shoots that forms the vascular tissue.

Proglottids

One of the segments of a tapeworm, containing both male and female reproductive organs

Prokaryotes

Prokaryotes are a group of organisms that lack a cell nucleus, or any other membrane-bound organelles.

Producer, in ecological systems

An autotrophic organism, usually a photosynthesizer, that contributes to the net primary productivity of a community.

Progesterone

Asteroid hormone secreted by the corpus luteum of the ovary; maintains the uterine lining during pregnancy.

Programmed cell death

Programmed cell death (PCD) is the suicide of a cell in a multicellular organism.

Prokaryotic cells

A type of cell lacking a membrane-enclosed nucleus and membrane-enclosed organelles; found only in the domains Bacteria and Archaea.

Prometaphase

The phase of mitosis in which the nuclear envelope breaks into fragments. Some of the spindle fibres reach the chromosomes and attach to protein structures at the centromeres, called kinetochores, while others make contact with microtubules coming from the opposite pole. The opposing spindle fibres move the chromosomes toward the metaphase plate, an imaginary plane equidistant from the poles.

Promoter

A specific nucleotide sequence in DNA that binds RNA polymerase and indicates where to start transcribing RNA.

Prophage

A phage genome that has been inserted into a specific site on the bacterial chromosome.

Prophase

The first stage of mitosis, during which duplicated chromosomes condense from chromatin, and the mitotic spindle forms and begins moving the chromosomes toward the centre of the cell.

Proplastids

An immature, colourless plastid. Proplastids occur in the cells of meristematic tissues. They consist of a double membrane enclosing granular stroma, multiply by division, and give rise in mature cells to leucoplasts or chromoplasts.

Prop roots

A root that grows from and supports the stem above the ground in plants such as mangroves.

Prosimian

A lower primate; includes lemurs, lorises, tarsiers, and bush babies, as well as many fossil forms.

Prostaglandin

One of a group of modified fatty acids secreted by virtually all tissues and performing a wide variety of functions as messengers.

Prostate gland

A gland in human males that secretes an acid-neutralizing component of semen.

Proteins

A three-dimensional biological polymer constructed from a set of 20 different monomers called amino acids.

Protein kinase

An enzyme that transfers phosphate groups from ATP to a protein.

Protein phosphatase

An enzyme that removes phosphate groups from proteins, often functioning to reverse the effect of a protein kinase.

Proteoglycans

A glycoprotein in the extracellular matrix of animal cells, rich in carbohydrate.

Proteasome

A giant protein complex that recognizes and destroys proteins tagged for elimination by the small protein ubiquitin.

Protistans

Any of a group of eukaryotic organisms belonging to the kingdom Protista according to some widely used modern taxonomic systems. The protists include a variety of unicellular, coenocytic, colonial, and multicellular organisms, such as the protozoans, slime moulds, brown algae, and red algae.

Prosthetic group

The nonprotein component of a conjugated protein, as the heme group in haemoglobin.

Protista

A kingdom into which all organisms of the simple biological organization can be classified. It includes algae, bacteria, fungi, and protozoa.

Protoderm

The outermost primary meristem, which gives rise to the epidermis of roots and shoots.

Proton

A subatomic particle with a single positive electrical charge, found in the nucleus of the atom.

Protonephridia.

The ciliated excretory tube that is specialized for filtration.

Proton-motive force

The potential energy stored in the form of an electrochemical gradient, generated by the pumping of hydrogen ions across biological membranes during chemiosmosis.

Proton pump

An active transport mechanism in cell membranes that consumes ATP to force hydrogen ions out of a cell and, in the process, generates a membrane potential.

Protonema

The green filamentous growth that arises from spore germination in liverworts and mosses and eventually gives rise to a mature gametophyte.

Protonephridium

An excretory system, such as the flame-cell system of flatworms, consisting of a network of closed tubules having external openings called nephridiopores and lacking internal openings.

Proto-oncogene

A normal cellular gene corresponding to an oncogene; a gene with a potential to cause cancer, but that requires some alteration to become an oncogene.

Protoplasm

The colloidal and liquid substance of which cells are formed, excluding horny, chitinous, and other structural material; the cytoplasm and nucleus.

Protoplast

The contents of a plant cell exclusive of the cell wall.

Protostome

A member of one of two distinct evolutionary lines of coelomates, consisting of the annelids, molluscs, and arthropods, and characterized by spiral, determinate cleavage, the schizocoelous formation of the coelom, and development of the mouth from the blastopore.

Protozoan

A protist that lives primarily by ingesting food, an animal-like mode of nutrition.

Prototherians

Warm-blooded vertebrates characterized by mammary glands in the female.

Protrusible

Capable of being thrust forward, as the tongue

Provirus

Viral DNA that inserts into a host genome.

Proximate causation

The hypothesis about why natural selection favoured a particular animal behaviour.

Pseudocolour

A body cavity consisting of a fluid-filled space between the endoderm and the mesoderm; characteristic of the nematodes.

Pseudocoelomate

An animal, such as a rotifer or roundworm, whose body cavity is not completely lined by mesoderm.

Pseudopodium

A cellular extension of amoeboid cells used in moving and feeding.

Pteridophyta

A division of the plant kingdom that includes the ferns, horsetails, and clubmosses.

Pyrenoid

A proteinaceous structure found within the chloroplast of certain algae and hornworts. It is considered to be associated with starch deposition.

Pulmocutaneous arteries

About the lungs and the akin; as, the *pulmocutaneous* arteries of the frog.

Pulmonary

About the lungs.

Pulmonary artery

In birds and mammals, an artery that carries deoxygenated blood from the right ventricle of the heart to the lungs, where it is oxygenated.

Pulmonary vein

In birds and mammals, a vein that carries oxygenated blood from the lungs to the left atrium of the heart, from which blood is pumped into the left ventricle and from there to the body tissues.

Plumule

Down feather of young birds; persists in some adult birds

Pulse

Measurement of heart rate; distention of an artery that can be felt each time the heart contracts.

Pulvinus

A cushionlike swelling at the base of the stalk of a leaf or leaflet.

Punctuated equilibrium

A theory of evolution advocating spurts of relatively rapid change followed by long periods of stasis.

Punnett square

The checkerboard diagram used for the analysis of allele segregation.

Pupa

A developmental stage of some insects, in which the organism is nonfeeding, immotile, and sometimes encapsulated or in a cocoon; the pupal stage occurs between the larval and adult phases.

Purine

A nitrogenous base, such as adenine or guanine, with a characteristic two-ring structure; one of the components of nucleic acids.

pyramid

An ancient monumental structure constructed of or faced with stone or brick and having a rectangular base and four sloping triangular sides meeting at an apex.

Pyramid of energy

A diagram of the energy flow between the trophic levels of an ecosystem; plants or other autotrophs (at the base of the pyramid) represent the greatest amount of energy, herbivores next, then primary carnivores, secondary carnivores, etc.

Pyrimidine

A nitrogenous base, such as cytosine, thymine, or uracil, with a characteristic single-ring structure; one of the components of nucleic acids.

Q

Quantitative character

A heritable feature in a population that varies continuously as a result of environmental influences and the additive effect of two or more genes (polygenic inheritance).

Quaternary structure

The particular shape of a complex, aggregate protein, defined by the characteristic three- dimensional arrangement of its constituent subunits, each a polypeptide.

Queen

In social insects (ants, termites, and some species of bees and wasps), the fertile, or fully developed, a female whose function is to lay eggs.

Quiescent centre

A region located within the zone of cell division in plant roots, containing meristematic cells that divide very slowly.

Quincuncial

Of, relating to, or forming a quincunx.

R

R plasmid

A bacterial plasmid carrying genes that confer resistance to certain antibiotics.

R-selection

The concept that in certain (r-selected) populations, a high reproductive rate is the chief determinant of life history.

Racemose

Having stalked flowers along an elongated stem that continue to open in succession from below as the stem continues to grow; "lilies of the valley are racemose".

Radial

The primary cylinder of vascular bundles is as a rule composed of radially located xylem elements and peripheral phloem.

Radial cleavage

A type of embryonic development in deuterostomes in which the planes of cell division that transform the zygote into a ball of cells are either parallel or perpendicular to the polar axis, thereby aligning tiers of cells one above the other.

Radially symmetrical

The property of symmetry about an axis.

Radial symmetry

Characterizing a body shaped like a pie or a barrel, with many equal parts radiating outward like the spokes of a wheel; present in cnidarians and echinoderms.

Radiation

The energy emitted in the form of waves or particles.

Radiata

Members of the radially symmetrical animal phyla, including cnidarians.

Radicle

An embryonic root of a plant.

Radioactive dating

A method of determining the age of fossils and rocks using half-lives of radioactive isotopes.

Radioactive isotope

An isotope, an atomic form of a chemical element, that is unstable; the nucleus decays spontaneously, giving off detectable particles and energy.

Radiometric dating

A method palaeontologists use for determining the ages of rocks and fossils on a scale of absolute time, based on the half-life of radioactive isotopes.

Radio-ulna

A single bone in the forelimb of an amphibian (as a frog) that represents a fusion of the separate radius and ulna of higher vertebrate forms

Raphids

One of a bundle of needlelike crystals of calcium oxalate occurring in many plant cells.

Reactant

A starting material in a chemical reaction.

Receptor

On or in a cell, a specific protein molecule whose shape fits that of a specific molecular messenger, such as a hormone.

Receptor-mediated endocytosis

The movement of specific molecules into a cell by the inward budding of membranous vesicles containing proteins with receptor sites specific to the molecules being taken in; enables a cell to acquire bulk quantities of specific substances.

Receptor potential

An initial response of a receptor cell to a stimulus, consisting of a change in voltage across the receptor membrane proportional to the stimulus strength. The intensity of the receptor potential determines the frequency of action potentials travelling to the nervous system.

Recessive allele

In a heterozygote, the allele that is completely masked in the phenotype.

Reciprocal altruism

Altruistic behaviour between unrelated individuals; believed to produce some benefit to the altruistic individual in the future when the current beneficiary reciprocates.

Recognition sequence

A specific sequence of nucleotides at which a restriction enzyme cleaves a DNA molecule.

Recognition species concept

The idea that specific mating adaptations become fixed in a population and form the basis of species identification.

Recombinant

An offspring whose phenotype differs from that of the parents.

Recombinant DNA

A DNA molecule made in vitro with segments from different sources.

Recombination

The formation of new gene combinations; in eukaryotes, may be accomplished by new associations of chromosomes produced during sexual reproduction or crossing over; in prokaryotes, may be accomplished through transformation, conjugation, or transduction.

Recombinase

An enzyme that catalyzes genetic recombination.

Red blood corpuscles

A cell in the blood of vertebrates that transports oxygen and carbon dioxide to and from the tissues. In mammals, the red blood cell is disk-shaped and biconcave, contains haemoglobin, and lacks a nucleus. Also called *erythrocyte*, *red cell*; Also called *red corpuscle*.

Redox reaction

A chemical reaction involving the transfer of one or more electrons from one reactant to another; also called oxidation-reduction reaction.

Reducing agent

The electron donor in a redox reaction.

Reduction

The gaining of electrons by a substance involved in a redox reaction.

Reflex

An automatic reaction to a stimulus, mediated by the spinal cord or lower brain.

Refractory period

The short time immediately after an action potential in which the neuron cannot respond to another stimulus, owing to an increase in potassium permeability.

Regeneration

The act or process of regenerating or the state of being regenerated.

Regulative development

A pattern of development, such as that of a mammal, in which the early blastomeres retain the potential to form the entire animal.

Relative fitness

The contribution of one genotype to the next generation compared to that of alternative genotypes for the same locus.

Relay neuron

The neuron that transmits signals between different regions of the central nervous system.

Releaser

A signal stimulus that functions as a communication signal between individuals of the same species.

Releasing hormone

A hormone produced by neurosecretory cells in the hypothalamus of the vertebrate brain that stimulates or inhibits the secretion of hormones by the anterior pituitary.

Renal

About the kidney.

Retrovirus

Retrovirus is a family of viruses that can affect the gastrointestinal system and respiratory tract.

Repetitive DNA

Nucleotide sequences, usually noncoding, that are present in many copies in a eukaryotic genome. The repeated units may be short and arranged tandemly (in series) or long and dispersed in the genome.

Replication

The process of making a copy of something.

Replication fork

A Y-shaped point on a replicating DNA molecule where new strands are growing.

Repressible enzyme

An enzyme whose synthesis is inhibited by a specific metabolite.

Repressor

A protein that suppresses the transcription of a gene.

Reproduction

The act of reproducing or the condition or process of being reproduced.

Reproductive isolation

Two populations of organisms are isolated if their members are unable to interbreed and produce fertile offspring. Various structural, behavioural, and biochemical features can prevent interbreeding and thus reproductively isolate populations as distinct species.

Reptilia

The vertebrate class of reptiles, represented by lizards, snakes, turtles, and crocodilian

Reptile

Any of various cold-blooded, usually egg-laying vertebrates of the class Reptilia, such as a snake, lizard, crocodile, turtle, or dinosaur, having an external covering of scales or horny plates and breathing through lungs.

Resins

A solid or semisolid substance obtained from certain plants.

Resolving power

A measure of the clarity of an image; the minimum distance that two points can be separated and still be distinguished as two separate points.

Resource partitioning

The division of environmental resources by coexisting species populations such that the niche of each species differs by one or more significant factors from the niches of all coexisting species populations.

Respiration

In aerobic organisms, the intake of oxygen and the liberation of carbon dioxide. In cells, the oxygen-requiring stage in the breakdown and release of energy from fuel molecules.

Resting potential

The membrane potential characteristic of a nonconducting, excitable cell, with the inside of the cell more negative than the outside.

Restriction enzyme

A degradative enzyme that recognizes and cuts up DNA (including that of certain phages) that is foreign to a bacterium.

Restriction fragment length polymorphisms (RFLPs)

Differences in the DNA sequence on homologous chromosomes that result in different patterns of restriction fragment lengths (DNA segments resulting from treatment with restriction enzymes); useful as genetic markers for making linkage maps.

Restriction site

A specific sequence on a DNA strand that is recognized as a "cut site" by a restriction enzyme.

Respiratory

Affecting respiration.

Reticular formation

A brain circuit involved with alertness and direction of attention to selected events; consists of a loose network of interneurons running through the brainstem, plus certain neurons in the thalamus that function as an extension of this network.

Retina

The innermost layer of the vertebrate eye, containing photoreceptor cells (rods and cones) and neurons; transmits images formed by the lens to the brain via the optic nerve.

Retinal

The light-absorbing pigment in rods and cones of the vertebrate eye.

Retrovirus

An RNA virus that reproduces by transcribing its RNA into DNA and then inserting the DNA into a cellular chromosome; an important class of cancer-causing viruses.

Reverse transcriptase

An enzyme encoded by some RNA viruses that use RNA as a template for DNA synthesis.

Rhizoid

Rootlike anchoring structure in fungi and nonvascular plants.

Rhizodermis

Rhizodermis is the root epidermis (also referred to as **epiblem**), the outermost primary cell layer of the root.

Rhizome

In vascular plants, a horizontal stem growing along or below the surface of the soil; maybe enlarged for storage or may function in vegetative reproduction.

Rhodopsin

A visual pigment consisting of retinal and opsin. When rhodopsin absorbs light, the retinal changes shape and dissociates from the opsin, after which it is converted back to its original form.

Ribonucleic acid (RNA)

A type of nucleic acid consisting of nucleotide monomers with a ribose sugar and the nitrogenous bases adenine (A), cytosine (C), guanine (G), and uracil (U); usually single-stranded; functions in protein synthesis and as the genome of some viruses.

Ribose

 The sugar component of RNA.

Ribosomal RNA (rRNA)

The most abundant type of RNA. Together with proteins, it forms the structure of ribosomes that coordinate the sequential coupling of tRNA molecules to the series of mRNA codons.

Ribonucleoprotein

A nucleoprotein that contains RNA.

Ribosome

A cell organelle constructed in the nucleolus, functioning as the site of protein synthesis in the cytoplasm. Consists of rRNA and protein molecules, which make up two subunits.

Ribozyme

An enzymatic RNA molecule that catalyzes reactions during RNA splicing.

Right atrium

The right upper chamber of the heart that receives blood from the venae cavae and coronary sinus

RNA

Abbreviation of ribonucleic acid.

RNA polymerase

An enzyme that links together the growing chain of ribonucleotides during transcription.

RNA processing

Modification of RNA before it leaves the nucleus, a process unique to eukaryotes.

RNA splicing

The removal of noncoding portions (introns) of the RNA molecule after initial synthesis.

Rod cell

One of two kinds of photoreceptors in the vertebrate retina; sensitive to black and white and enables night vision.

Rosette manner

An ornament or badge made of ribbon or silk that is pleated or gathered to resemble a rose and is used to decorate clothing or is worn in the buttonhole of civilian dress to

Root

The descending axis of a plant, normally below ground and serving both to anchor the plant and to take up and conduct water and dissolved minerals.

Root cap

A cone of cells at the tip of a plant root that protects the apical meristem.

Rotifers

A class of the phylum Aschelminthes distinguished by the corona, a retractile trochal disk provided with several groups of cilia and located on the head.

Root hair

A tiny projection growing just behind the root tips of plants, increasing surface area for the absorption of water and minerals.

Root pressure

The upward push of water within the stele of vascular plants, caused by active pumping of minerals into the xylem by root cells.

Rough ER

That portion of the endoplasmic reticulum studded with ribosomes.

Rubisco

Ribulose carboxylase, the enzyme that catalyzes the first step (the addition of CO_2 to RuBP, or ribulose bisphosphate) of the Calvin cycle.

Ruminant

An animal, such as a cow or a sheep, with an elaborate, multi compartmentalized stomach specialized for a herbivorous diet.

Runner

One who competes in a race.

S

Sacral

Near, or relating to the sacrum.

Salamander

Any of various small lizardlike amphibians of the order Caudata, having porous scaleless skin and four, often weak or rudimentary legs.

S phase

The synthesis phase of the cell cycle, constituting the portion of interphase during which DNA is replicated.

SA (sinoatrial) node

The pacemaker of the heart, located in the wall of the right atrium. At the base of the wall separating the two atria is another patch of nodal tissue called the atrioventricular node (AV).

Sacral

Of, near, or relating to the sacrum.

Saltatory conduction

Rapid transmission of a nerve impulse along an axon resulting from the action potential jumping from one node of Ranvier to another, skipping the myelin-sheathed regions of the membrane.

Saprobe

An organism that acts as a decomposer by absorbing nutrients from dead organic matter.

Sarcolemma

The specialized plasma membrane surrounding a muscle cell (muscle fibre); capable of propagating action potentials.

Sarcomere

The fundamental, repeating unit of striated muscle, delimited by the Z lines.

Sarcoplasmic reticulum

A modified form of endoplasmic reticulum in striated muscle cells that stores calcium used to trigger contraction during stimulation.

Satellites

In genetics, a knob of chromatin connected by a stalk to the short arm of certain chromosomes.

Saturated fatty acid

A fatty acid in which all carbons in the hydrocarbon tail are connected by single bonds, thus maximizing the number of hydrogen atoms that can attach to the carbon skeleton.

Savanna

A tropical grassland biome with scattered individual trees, large herbivores, and three distinct seasons based primarily on rainfall, maintained by occasional fires and drought.

Schizocoelus

The type of development found in protosomes. Initially solid masses of mesoderm split to form coelomic cavities.

Schwann cells

A chain of supporting cells enclosing the axons of many neurons and forming an insulating layer called the myelin sheath.

Sclereids

A short, irregular sclerenchyma cell in nutshells and seed coats and scattered through the parenchyma of some plants.

Sclerenchyma cell

A rigid, supportive plant cell type usually lacking protoplasts and possessing thick secondary walls strengthened by lignin at maturity.

Scolex

The knoblike anterior end of a tapeworm, having suckers or hooklike parts that in the adult stage serve as organs of attachment to the host on which the tapeworm is parasitic.

Scute

A horny, chitinous, or bony external plate or scale, as on the shell of a turtle or the underside of a snake. Also called a *scutum*.

Scutellum

A shield-like bony plate or scale, as on the thorax of some insects.

Sebaceous glands

The small glands in the skin that secrete oil into hair follicles and onto most of the body surface.

The second law of thermodynamics

The principle whereby every energy transfer or transformation increases the entropy of the universe. Ordered forms of energy are at least partly converted to heat, and in spontaneous reactions, the free energy of the system also decreases.

Second messenger

A small, nonprotein, water-soluble molecule or ion, such as calcium ion or cyclic AMP, that relays a signal to a cell's interior in response to a signal received by a signal receptor protein.

Secondary meristem

In flowering plants, meristems develop from cells that suspend their ability to divide and resume this activity later. Such meristems are known as secondary meristems. These cells give rise to permanent secondary tissues.

Secondary cell wall

The innermost wall of a plant cell that is deposited after cell elongation has enclosed.

Secondary compound

A chemical compound synthesized through the diversion of products of major metabolic pathways for use in defence by prey species.

Secondary consumer

A member of the trophic level of an ecosystem consisting of carnivores that eat herbivores.

Secondary growth

The increase in girth of the stems and roots of many plants, especially woody, perennial dicots.

Secondary immune response

The immune response elicited when an animal encounters the same antigen at some later time. The secondary immune response is more rapid, of greater magnitude, and of longer duration than the primary immune response.

Secondary productivity

He rate at which all the heterotrophs in an ecosystem incorporate organic material into new biomass, which can be equated to chemical energy.

Secondary rachis

A large compound leaf of a palm.

Secondary sex characteristics

Characteristics of animals that distinguish between the two sexes but that do not produce or convey gametes; includes facial hair of the human male and enlarged hips and breasts of the female.

Secondary structure

The localized, repetitive coiling or folding of the polypeptide backbone of a protein due to hydrogen bond formation between peptide linkages.

Secondary succession

A type of succession that occurs where an existing community has been severely cleared by some disturbance.

Secretion

(1)   The discharge of molecules synthesized by the cell.

(2)   In the vertebrate kidney, the discharge of wastes from the blood into the filtrate from the nephron tubules.

Secretory tissue

Secretory tissue in the interior of the gland is made up of Secretory tissue - This is made up of secretory epithelial cells.

Secondary cell wall

The secondary cell wall is a structure found in many plant cells, located between the primary cell wall and the plasma membrane. The cell starts producing the secondary cell wall only after the primary cell wall is complete and the cell has stopped growing.

Secondary xylem

Xylem produced by cambium, composed of two interpenetrating systems, the horizontal (ray) and vertical (axial).

Sedimentary rock

Rock formed from sand and mud that once settled in layers on the bottom of seas, lakes, and marshes. Sedimentary rocks are often rich in fossils.

Seed

An adaptation for terrestrial plants consisting of an embryo packaged along with a store of food within a resistant coat.

Segmentation

The subdivision of an organism or an organ into more or less equivalent parts.

Segregation

The separation of paired alleles during meiosis so that members of each pair of alleles appear in different gametes.

Selection

The process by which the forms of organisms in a population that are better adapted to the environmental conditions increase in frequency relative to less well-adapted forms over many generations.

Selection coefficient

The difference between two fitness values, representing a relative measure of selection against an inferior genotype.

Selective permeability

A property of biological membranes that allows some substances to cross more easily than others.

Selective pressure

An environmental factor that favours the survival and reproduction of those genetic variants within a population that is better adapted to the environment.

Self-incompatibility

The capability of certain flowers to block fertilization by pollen from the same or a closely related plant.

Biologynary

Self-fertilization

The union of egg and sperm produced by a single hermaphroditic organism.

Self-pollination

The transfer of pollen from the anther to stigma in the same flower or another flower of the same plant, leading to self-fertilization.

Semen

The fluid that is ejaculated by the male during orgasm; contains sperm and secretions from several glands of the male reproductive tract.

Semicircular canals

A three-part chamber of the inner ear that functions in maintaining equilibrium.

Semilunar valve

A valve located at the two exits of the heart, where the aorta leaves the left ventricle and the pulmonary artery leaves the right ventricle.

Seminal vesicle

A gland in males that secretes a fluid (a component of semen) that lubricates and nourishes sperm.

Seminiferous tubules

Highly coiled tubes in the testes in which sperm are produced.

Sensation

An impulse sent to the brain from activated receptors and sensory neurons.

Sensory neuron

A nerve cell that receives information from the internal and external environments and transmits the signals to the central nervous system.

Sensory receptor

A specialized structure that responds to specific stimuli from an animal's external or internal environment; transmits the information of an environmental stimulus to the animal's nervous system by converting stimulus energy to the electrochemical energy of action potentials.

Sepal

A whorl of modified leaves in angiosperms that encloses and protects the flower bud before it opens.

Septate

Divided by a septum or septa

Septum

A partition, or cross wall, that divides a structure, such as a fungal hypha, into compartments.

Sessile

Attached; not free to move about.

Sex chromosomes

The pair of chromosomes responsible for determining the sex of an individual.

Sex-linked genes

Genes located on one sex chromosome but not the other.

Sex-linked trait

An inherited trait, such as colour discrimination, determined by a gene located on a sex chromosome and that, therefore, shows a different pattern of inheritance in males and females.

Sexual dimorphism

A special case of polymorphism based on the distinction between the secondary sex characteristics of males and females.

Sexual reproduction

A type of reproduction in which two parents give rise to offspring that have unique combinations of genes inherited from the gametes of the two parents.

Sexual selection

Selection based on variation in secondary sex characteristics, leading to the enhancement of sexual dimorphism.

Shark

A person regarded as ruthless, greedy, or dishonest.

Shoot system

The aerial portion of a plant body, consisting of stems, leaves, and flowers.

Short-day plant

A plant that flowers, usually in late summer, fall, or winter, only when the light period is shorter than a critical length.

Sieve tube member

A chain of living cells that form sieve tubes in the phloem.

Sign stimulus

An external sensory stimulus that triggers a fixed action pattern.

Signal peptide

A stretch of amino acids on polypeptides that targets proteins to specific destinations in eukaryotic cells.

Signal-transduction pathway

A mechanism linking a mechanical or chemical stimulus to a cellular response.

Simple squamous epithelium

Epithelium made up of a single layer of flattened scale-like cells.

simple tissues

A simple tissue is composed of only a single kind of cell, while a complex tissue is composed of two or more different kinds of cells. In this week's lab, you will be introduced to the principal simple tissues of the plant body

Sink habitat

A habitat where mortality exceeds reproduction.

Sinoatrial node

Area of the vertebrate heart that initiates the heartbeat; located where the superior vena cava enters the right atrium; the pacemaker.

phoning

A pipe or tube fashioned or deployed in an inverted U shape and filled until atmospheric pressure is sufficient to force a liquid from a reserve

Sister chromatids

Replicated forms of a chromosome joined together by the centromere and eventually separated during mitosis or meiosis II.

Skeletal

The bodily system that consists of the bones, their associated cartilages, and the joints, and supports and protects the body, produces blood cells, and stores minerals.

Skeletal muscle

Striated muscle is generally responsible for the voluntary movements of the body.

Sliding-filament model

The theory explaining how muscle contracts, based on change within a sarcomere, the basic unit of muscle organization, stating that thin (actin) filaments slide across thick (myosin) filaments, shortening the sarcomere; the shortening of all sarcomeres in a myofibril shortens the entire myofibril.

Slime fungi

A group of small simple organisms widely distributed in damp habitats on land. They exist either as free cells or as multinucleate aggregates of cells.

Slime layer

A slime layer in bacteria is an easily removed, diffuse, unorganized layer of extracellular material that surround bacteria cells.

Small nuclear ribonucleoprotein (snRNP)

One of a variety of small particles in the cell nucleus, composed of RNA and protein molecules; functions are not fully understood, but some form parts of spliceosomes, active in RNA splicing.

Smooth ER

That portion of the endoplasmic reticulum that is free of ribosomes.

Smooth muscle

A type of muscle lacking the striations of skeletal and cardiac muscle because of the uniform distribution of myosin filaments in the cell.

Social dominance

A hierarchical pattern of social organization involving domination of some members of a group by other members in a relatively orderly and long-lasting pattern.

Society

An organization of individuals of the same species in which there are divisions of resources, divisions of labour, and mutual dependence; a society is held together by stimuli exchanged among members of the group.

Sociobiology

The study of social behaviour based on evolutionary theory.

Sodium-potassium pump

A special transport protein in the plasma membrane of animal cells that transports sodium out of and potassium into the cell against their concentration gradients.

Solids

Of definite shape and volume; not liquid or gaseous.

Solitary

Existing, living, or going without others; alone.

Solute

A substance that is dissolved in a solution.

Solution

A homogeneous, liquid mixture of two or more substances.solvent The dissolving agent of a solution. Water is the most versatile solvent known.

Somatic cell

Any cell in a multicellular organism except a sperm or egg cell.

Somatic (body) chromosomes

Any chromosome that is not a sex chromosome; appear in pairs in body cells but as single chromosomes in spermatozoa.

Somatic division

The process of cell division in sexually reproducing organisms that reduces the number of chromosomes in reproductive cells from diploid to haploid, leading to the production of gametes in animals and spores in plants.

Somatic nervous system

The branch of the motor division of the vertebrate peripheral nervous system composed of motor neurons that carry signals to skeletal muscles in response to external stimuli.

Somatoplasm

The protoplasm of a somatic cell.

Somatotropin

A hormone, produced by the pituitary gland, that stimulates protein synthesis and promotes the growth of bone; also known as growth hormone.

Source habitat

A habitat where reproduction exceeds mortality and from which excess individuals disperse.

Southern blotting

A hybridization technique that enables researchers to determine the presence of certain nucleotide sequences in a sample of DNA.

Spathe

A large leaf that surrounds the base of a flower cluster.

A leaflike bract that encloses or subtends a flower cluster or spadix, as in the jack-in-the-pulpit and the calla.

Specialized

Of cells, having particular functions in a multicellular organism.

Speciation

The origin of new species in evolution.

Species

A particular kind of organism; members possess similar anatomical characteristics and have the ability to interbreed.

Species diversity

The number and relative abundance of species in a biological community.

Species richness

The number of species in a biological community.

Species selection

A theory maintaining that species living the longest and generating the greatest number of species determine the direction of major evolutionary trends.

Species-specific

Characteristic of a particular species.

Specific

Unique; for example, the proteins in a given organism, the enzyme catalyzing a given reaction, or the antibody to a given antigen.

Specific heat

The amount of heat that must be absorbed or lost for 1 g of a substance to change its temperature 1°C.

Spectrophotometer

An instrument that measures the proportions of light of different wavelengths absorbed and transmitted by a pigment solution.

Sperm

A male gamete.

Spermatid

Each of four haploid cells resulting from the meiotic divisions of a spermatocyte; each spermatid becomes differentiated into a sperm cell.

Spermatocytes

The diploid (2*n*) cells formed by the enlargement and differentiation of the spermatogonia; they give rise by meiotic division to the spermatids.

Spermatogonia

The unspecialized diploid (2*n*) cells on the walls of the seminiferous tubules that, by enlargement, differentiation, and meiotic division, become spermatocytes, then spermatids, then sperm cells.

Spermatogenesis

The continuous and prolific production of mature sperm cells in the testis.

S phase

The phase of the mitotic cycle during which DNA synthesis occurs.

Sphenodon

Either of two nocturnal lizardlike reptiles *(Sphenodon punctatus* or *S. guntheri)* that are found only on certain islands off New Zealand and are the only extant members of the Rhynchocephalia, an order that flourished during the Mesozoic Era. Also called *sphenodon.*

Sphingosine

A basic, long-chain, unsaturated amino alcohol, $C_{18}H_{37}NO_2$, found combined with lipids in the brain and tissue.

Sphincter

A ringlike valve, consisting of modified muscles in a muscular tube, such as a digestive tract; closes off the tube like a drawstring.

Spicule

A needlelike structure or part, such as one of the mineral structures supporting the soft tissue of certain invertebrates, especially sponges.

Spinal cord

Part of the vertebrate central nervous system; consists of a thick, dorsal, longitudinal bundle of nerve fibres extending posteriorly from the brain.

Spindle

An assemblage of microtubules that orchestrates chromosome movement during eukaryotic cell division.

Spine

Any of various pointed projections, processes, or appendages of animals.

Spiracle

One of the external openings of the respiratory system in terrestrial arthropods.

Spiral cleavage

A type of embryonic development in protostomes, in which the planes of cell division that transform the zygote into a ball of cells occur obliquely to the polar axis, resulting in cells of each tier sitting in the grooves between cells of adjacent tiers.

Spirilla

Any of various aerobic bacteria of the genus *Spirillum,* having an elongated spiral form and bearing a tuft of flagella.

Spleen

A large, highly vascular lymphoid organ, lying in the human body to the left of the stomach below the diaphragm, serving to store blood, disintegrate old blood cells, filter foreign substances from the blood, and produce lymphocytes.

Spliceosome

A complex assembly that interacts with the ends of an RNA intron in splicing RNA; releases an intron and joins two adjacent exons.

Springwood

Young, usually softwood that lies directly beneath the bark and develops in early spring.

Spirochetes

Any bacterium of the genus *Spirochaeta* that is motile and spiral-shaped with flexible filaments. Spirochetes include the organisms responsible for leprosy, relapsing fever, syphilis, and yaws.

Spongocoel

The central cavity of a sponge, which opens to the outside by way of the osculum.

Spongy parenchyma

In-plant leaves, a tissue composed of loosely arranged chloroplast-containing parenchyma cells.

Sporophyll

A leaf or leaflike organ that bears spores.

Sporangiophore

A specialized hypha or a branch bearing one or more sporangia.

Sporangium

A capsule in fungi and plants in which meiosis occurs and haploid spores develop.

Spore

In the life cycle of a plant or alga undergoing alternation of generations, a meiotically produced haploid cell that divides mitotically, generating a multicellular individual, the gametophyte, without fusing with another cell.

Sporophyte

The multicellular diploid form in organisms undergoing alternation of generations that results from a union of gametes and that meiotically produces haploid spores that grow into the gametophyte generation.

Spongy parenchyma

A leaf tissue consisting of loosely arranged, chloroplast-bearing, usually lobed cells. Also called *spongy parenchyma*.

Sporopollenin

A secondary product, a polymer synthesized by a side branch of a major metabolic pathway of plants that is resistant to almost all kinds of environmental damage; especially important in the evolutionary move of plants onto land.

Stabilizing selection

The natural selection that favours intermediate variants by acting against extreme phenotypes.

Stalks

A slender or elongated support or structure, as one that connects or supports an organ.

Stamen

The pollen-producing male reproductive organ of a flower, consisting of an anther and filament.

Staminode

A sterile stamen, sometimes resembling a petal, as in the canna.

Starch

A storage polysaccharide in plants consisting entirely of glucose.

Statocyst

A type of mechanoreceptor that functions in equilibrium in invertebrates through the use of statoliths, which stimulate hair cells about gravity.

Statocysts

A small organ of balance in many invertebrates, consisting of a fluid-filled sac containing statoliths that stimulate sensory cells and help indicate position when the animal moves. also called otocyst.

Statoliths.

A granule of the statoconia.

Stele

The central vascular cylinder in roots where xylem and phloem are located.

Stem

The aboveground part of the axis of vascular plants, as well as anatomically similar portions below ground (such as rhizomes).

Stem cells

The common, self-regenerating cells in the marrow of long bones that give rise, by differentiation and division, to red blood cells and all of the different types of white blood cells.

Stratified squamous epithelium

A multiple-layered epithelium composed of thin, flat superficial cells and cuboidal and columnar deeper cells

Stereoisomer

A molecule that is a mirror image of another molecule with the same molecular formula.

Stereoscopic vision

Ability to perceive a single, three-dimensional image from the simultaneous but separate images delivered to the brain by each eye.

Sterols

Any of various alcohols having the structure of a steroid, usually with a hydroxyl group(OH) attached to the third carbon atom. Sterols are found in the tissues of animals, plants, fungi, and yeasts and include cholesterol.

Steroids

A class of lipids characterized by a carbon skeleton consisting of four rings with various functional groups attached.

Sternum

A long flat bone in the front of the body, to which the collarbone and most of the ribs are attached.

Stigma

In plants, the region of a carpel serving as a receptive surface for pollen grains, which germinate on it.

Stilt roots

An aerial root.

Stimulus

Any internal or external change or signal that influences the activity of an organism or part of an organism.

Stolons

An above-ground prostrate stem that develops roots and leaves at nodes along its length,

e.g. couch grass.

Stoma

A microscopic pore surrounded by guard cells in the epidermis of leaves and stems that allows gas exchange between the environment and the interior of the plant.

Stomatal apparatus

A surgically constructed opening, especially one in the abdominal wall that permits the passage of waste after a colostomy or ileostomy.

Stomatal complex

A small aperture in the surface of a membrane

Stomochord

A hollow pouch of the gut found in the proboscis of hemichordates.

Storage parenchyma

The tissue characteristic of an organ, as distinguished from associated connective or supporting tissues.

Strategy

A group of related traits evolved under the influence of natural selection, that solves particular problems encountered by living organisms; often includes anatomical, physiological, and behavioural characteristics.

Striated muscle

Skeletal voluntary muscle and cardiac muscle. The name derives from the striped appearance, which reflects the arrangement of contractile elements.

Strict aerobe

An organism that can survive only in an atmosphere of oxygen, which is used in aerobic respiration.

Strict anaerobe

An organism that cannot survive in an atmosphere of oxygen. Other substances, such as sulfate or nitrate, are the terminal electron acceptors in the electron transport chains that generate their ATP.

Stroma

The fluid of the chloroplast surrounding the thylakoid membrane; involved in the synthesis of organic molecules from carbon dioxide and water.

Stomata

One of the minutes pores in the epidermis of a leaf or stem through which gases and water vapour pass. Also called *stomate*

Stromatolite

Rock made of banded domes of sediment in which are found the most ancient forms of life: prokaryotes dating back as far as 3.5 billion years.

Structural formula

A type of molecular notation in which the constituent atoms are joined by lines representing covalent bonds.

Structuralgene

A gene that codes for a polypeptide.

Style

In angiosperms, the stalk of a carpel, down which the pollen tube grows.

Stylet

Small needle-like appendage; especially the feeding organ of a tardigrade

Synapse

The junction across which a nerve impulse passes from an axon terminal to a neuron, muscle cell, or gland cell.

Syrinx

The vocal organ of a bird, consisting of thin vibrating muscles at or close to the division of the trachea into the bronchi.

subcutaneous lymph

The soft tissue immediately underlying the skin or epidermis.

Suberized

To cause to undergo suberization

Suberin

A waxy waterproof substance present in the cell walls of cork tissue in plants.

Submetacentric

Having the centromere near the centre but not in the middle, so that one arm is shorter than the other.

Suborganelle

The analysis of this sub organelle organisation of the cell requires techniques conserving the native state of the protein complexes. ...

Subsidiary cells

A plant epidermal cell that is associated with guard cells and differs morphologically from other epidermal cells. Also called an *accessory cell*.

Substrate

(1)   The substance on which an enzyme works.

(2)   The foundation to which an organism is attached.

Substrate-level phosphorylation

The formation of ATP by directly transferring a phosphate group to ADP from an intermediate substrate in catabolism.

Succession

Ecological succession.

Sucking

Draw into the mouth by creating a practical vacuum in the mouth "suck the poison from the place where the snake bit";

Suctorial

Adapted for sucking or clinging by suction

Sucrose

Cane sugar; a common disaccharide found in many plants; a molecule of glucose linked to a molecule of fructose.

Suctorial

Having organs or parts adapted for sucking or clinging.

Sugar

Any monosaccharide or disaccharide.

Suckers

An organ or other structure adapted for sucking nourishment or for clinging to objects by suction.

Summation

A phenomenon of neural integration in which the membrane potential of the postsynaptic cell in a chemical synapse is determined by the total activity of all excitatory and inhibitory presynaptic impulses acting on it at any one time.

Superior

Inserted or situated above the perianth. Used of an ovary.

Suppressor T cell (T_S)

A type of T cell that causes B cells as well as other cells to ignore antigens.

Suppressor genes

A gene that can reverse the effect of a specific kind of mutation in other genes.

Surface tension

A measure of how difficult it is to stretch or break the surface of a liquid. Water has a high surface tension because of the hydrogen bonding of surface molecules.

Survivorship curve

A plot of the number of members of a cohort that are still alive at each age; one way to represent age-specific mortality.

Suspension-feeder

An aquatic animal, such as a clam or a baleen whale, that sifts small food particles from the water.

Sustainable agriculture

Long-term productive farming methods that are environmentally safe.

Sustainable development

The long-term prosperity of human societies and the ecosystems that support them.

Swim bladder

An adaptation, derived from a lung, that enables bony fishes to adjust their density and thereby control their buoyancy.

Symbiont

The smaller participant in a symbiotic relationship, living in or on the host.

Symbiosis

An ecological relationship between organisms of two different species that live together in direct contact.

Sympathetic division

One of two divisions of the autonomic nervous system of vertebrates; generally increases energy expenditure and prepares the body for action.

Sympatric speciation

A mode of speciation occurring as a result of a radical change in the genome that produces a reproductively isolated subpopulation in its parent population.

Symplast

In plants, the continuum of cytoplasm connected by plasmodesmata between cells.

Synapomorphies

Shared derived characters; homologies that evolved in an ancestor common to all species on one branch of a fork in a cladogram, but not common to species on the other branch.

Synapse

The locus where one neuron communicates with another neuron in a neural pathway; a narrow gap between a synaptic terminal of an axon and a signal-receiving portion (dendrite or cell body) of another neuron or effector cell. Neurotransmitter molecules released by synaptic terminals diffuse across the synapse, relaying messages to the dendrite or effector.

Synapsis

The pairing of replicated homologous chromosomes during prophase I of meiosis.

Synaptic cleft

A narrow gap separating the synaptic knob of a transmitting neuron from a receiving neutron to an effector.

Synaptic knob

The relay point at the tip of a transmitting neuron's axon, where signals are sent to another neuron or an effector.

Synaptic terminal

A bulb at the end of an axon in which neurotransmitter molecules are stored and released.

Syncarpous

Having or consisting of united carpels. Used of a pistil.

Syncytial

Multinucleate mass of cytoplasm resulting from the fusion of cells.

Syngamy

The process of a cellular union during fertilization.

Synthesis

The formation of a more complex substance from simpler ones.

Synthesis phase

In the cell cycle, the phase in which the DNA of the chromosomes is replicated and DNA- associated proteins, such as histones, are synthesized.

Systematics

The branch of biology that studies the diversity of life; encompasses taxonomy and is involved in reconstructing phylogenetic history.

Systemic acquired resistance (SAR)

A defensive response in infected plants that helps protect healthy tissue from pathogenic invasion.

Systole

The stage of the heart cycle in which the heart muscle contracts and the chambers pump blood.

Systolic pressure

The pressure in an artery during the ventricular contraction phase of the heart cycle.

T

T cell

A type of lymphocyte responsible for cell-mediated immunity that differentiates under the influence of the thymus.

Tadpole

The limbless aquatic larva of a frog or toad, having gills and a long flat tail. As the tadpole approaches the adult stage, legs and lungs develop, and the tail gradually disappears. Also called *polliwog*.

Taiga

The coniferous or boreal forest biome, characterized by considerable snow, harsh winters, short summers, and evergreen trees.

Tannins

A yellowish compound found in many plants, such as tea and grapes, and used in tanning and dyeing also called tannic acid. (Or)

Any of various complex phenolic substances of plant origin; used in tanning and medicine.

Tapeworm

Any of various ribbonlike, often very long flatworms of the class Cestoda, that lack an alimentary canal and are parasitic in the intestines of vertebrates, including humans.

Tarsals

Elating to, or situated near the tarsus of the foot: *the tarsal bones.*

Taxis

A movement toward or away from a stimulus.

Taxon

The named taxonomic unit at any given level.

Taxonomy

The branch of biology concerned with naming and classifying the diverse forms of life.

Tegmen

A covering or integument, such as the tough leathery forewing of certain insects or the inner coat of a seed. Also called *tegmentum.*

Tegument

A natural outer covering; an integument.

Telomerase

An enzyme that catalyzes the lengthening of telomeres; the enzyme includes a molecule of RNA that serves as a template for new telomere segments.

Telomere

The protective structure at each end of a eukaryotic chromosome. Specifically, the tandemly repetitive DNA (*see* Repetitive DNA) at the end of the chromosome's DNA molecule.

Telophase

The fourth and final stage of mitosis, during which daughter nuclei form at the two poles of a cell. Telophase usually occurs together with cytokinesis.

Temperate bacteriophage

A bacterial virus that may become incorporated into the host cell chromosome.

Temperate deciduous forest

A biome located throughout mid-latitude regions where there is sufficient moisture to support the growth of large, broad-leaf deciduous trees.

Temperate virus

A virus that can reproduce without killing the host.

Temperature

A measure of the intensity of heat in degrees, reflecting the average kinetic energy of the molecules.

Template

A pattern or mould guiding the formation of a negative or complimentary copy.

Tendon

A type of fibrous connective tissue that attaches muscle to bone.

Tendril

A threadlike leaf or stem by which a climbing plant attaches itself to support. E.g. grape, cucumber.

Tentacles

Long, flexible protrusions located about the mouth of many invertebrates; usually prehensile or tactile.

Tentaculocyst

One of the auditory organs of certain medusa. It is also called auditory tentacle.

Tepal

A division of the perianth of a flower having a virtually indistinguishable calyx and corolla, as in tulips and lilies.

Terrestrial

Living on or in the ground; not aquatic, arboreal, or aerial.

Terminator

A special sequence of nucleotides in DNA that marks the end of a gene; it signals RNA polymerase to release the newly made RNA molecule, which then departs from the gene.

Terpenes

Terpenes commonly occur in the oils that give plants their fragrance. The fundamental building block of terpenes is the isoprene unit, C_5H_8.

Terpenoid compounds

Any compound with an isoprenoid structure similar to that of the terpene hydrocarbons.

Territory

An area or space occupied and defended by an individual or a group; trespassers are attacked (and usually defeated); maybe the site of breeding, nesting, food gathering, or any combination thereof.

Tertiary consumer

A member of a trophic level of an ecosystem consisting of carnivores that eat mainly other carnivores.

Tertiary structure

Irregular contortions of a protein molecule due to interactions of side chains involved in hydrophobic interactions, ionic bonds, hydrogen bonds, and disulfide bridges.

Testa

The protective outer layer of seeds of flowering plants

Testcross

Breeding of an organism of unknown genotype with a homozygous recessive individual to determine the unknown genotype. The ratio of phenotypes in the offspring determines the unknown genotype.

Testis

The male reproductive organ, or gonad, in which sperm and reproductive hormones are produced.

Testosterone

The most abundant androgen hormone in the male body.

Tetanus

The maximal, sustained contraction of a skeletal muscle, caused by a very fast frequency of action potentials elicited by continual stimulation.

Tetrad

In genetics, a pair of homologous chromosomes that have replicated and come together in prophase I of meiosis; consists of four chromatids.

Tetrapod

A vertebrate possessing two pairs of limbs, such as amphibians, reptiles, birds, and mammals.

Thalamus

One of two integrating centres of the vertebrate forebrain. Neurons with cell bodies in the thalamus relay neural input to specific areas in the cerebral cortex and regulate what information goes to the cerebral cortex.

Thallophyta

A former division of the plant kingdom containing relatively simple plants i.e, those with no leaves, stems, or roots. It included algae, bacteria, fungi, and lichens.

Thallus

A simple plant or algal body without true roots, leaves, or stems.

Theory

A generalization based on many observations and experiments; a verified hypothesis.

Thermodynamics

The study of transformations of energy. The first law of thermodynamics states that, in all processes, the total energy of a system plus its surroundings remains constant. The second law states that all natural processes tend to proceed in such a direction that the disorder or randomness of the system increases.

Thermoregulation

The maintenance of internal temperature within a tolerable range.

Thick filament

A filament composed of staggered arrays of myosin molecules; a component of myofibrils in muscle fibres.

Thigmomorphogenesis

A response in plants to chronic mechanical stimulation, resulting from increased ethylene production; an example is thickening stems in response to strong winds.

Thigmotropism

The directional growth of a plant with touch.

Thoracic

The part of the human body between the neck and the diaphragm, partially encased by the ribs and containing the heart and lungs; the chest.

Thorax

In vertebrates, that portion of the trunk containing the heart and lungs.

Thorns

A modified branch in the form of a sharp, woody spine.

Threatened species

Species that are likely to become endangered in the foreseeable future throughout all or a significant portion of their range.

Therians

Theria (′therēe) (vertebrate zoology) A subclass of the class Mammalia including all living mammals

Threshold potential

The potential an excitable cell membrane must reach for an action potential to be initiated.

Thorns

A modified branch in the form of a sharp, woody spine.

Thylakoids

A flattened membrane sac inside the chloroplast used to convert light energy to chemical energy.

Thymus

An endocrine gland in the neck region of mammals that is active in establishing the immune system; secretes several messengers, including thymosin, that stimulate T cells.

Thyroid gland

An endocrine gland that secretes iodine-containing hormones (T_3 and T_4), which stimulate metabolism and influence development and maturation in vertebrates, and calcitonin, which lowers blood calcium levels in mammals.

Thyroid-stimulating hormone (TSH)

A hormone produced by the anterior pituitary that regulates the release of thyroid hormones.

Tibia

The inner and larger of the two bones of the lower human leg, extending from the knee to the ankle.

Ti plasmid

A plasmid of a tumour-inducing bacterium that integrates a segment of its DNA into the host chromosome of a plant; frequently used as a carrier for genetic engineering in plants.

Tight junction

A type of intercellular junction in animal cells that prevents the leakage of material between cells.

Tissues

An integrated group of cells with a common structure and function.

Tonoplast

A membrane that encloses the central vacuole in a plant cell, separating the cytosol from the cell sap.

Torpor

In animals, a physiological state that conserves energy by slowing down the heart and respiratory systems.

Tornaria

The peculiar free-swimming larva of Balanoglossus.

Totipotency

The ability of embryonic cells to retain the potential to form all parts of the animal.

Trace element

An element indispensable for life but required in extremely minute amounts.

Trachea

The windpipe; that portion of the respiratory tube that has C-shaped cartilaginous rings and passes from the larynx to two bronchi.

Tracheophyta

A group (division) of the plant kingdom containing all plants possession is a vascular tissue.

Trachea

Tiny air tubes that branch throughout the insect body for gas exchange.

Tracheal system

A gas exchange system of branched, chitin-lined tubes that infiltrate the body and carry oxygen directly to cells in insects.

Tracheid

A water-conducting and the supportive element of xylem composed of long, thin cells with tapered ends and walls hardened with lignin.

Tract

A group or bundle of nerve fibres with accompanying connective tissue, located within the central nervous system.

Transcription

The synthesis of RNA on a DNA template.

Transcription factor

A regulatory protein that binds to DNA and stimulates transcription of specific genes.

Transduction

The transfer of genetic material (DNA) from one cell to another by a virus.

Transfer RNA (tRNA)

An RNA molecule that functions as an interpreter between nucleic acid and protein language by picking up specific amino acids and recognizing the appropriate codons in the mRNA.

Transformation

(1)   The conversion of a normal animal cell to a cancerous cell.

(2)   A phenomenon in which external DNA is assimilated by a cell.

Transgenic

Having artificially altered genetic material. A transgenic organism is one that has had its genotype altered by the introduction of a gene or DNA sequence into its genome by genetic manipulation; the introduced gene or DNA segment is called a transgene.

Translation

The synthesis of a polypeptide using the genetic information encoded in an mRNA molecule. There is a change of "language" from nucleotides to amino acids.

Translocation

(1)   An aberration in chromosome structure resulting from an error in meiosis or from mutagens; attachment of a chromosomal fragment to a nonhomologous chromosome.

(2)   During protein synthesis, the third stage in the elongation cycle when the RNA carrying the growing polypeptide moves from the A site to the P site on the ribosome. (3) The transport via phloem of food in a plant.

Transpiration

The evaporative loss of water from a plant.

Transposon

A transposable genetic element; a mobile segment of DNA that serves as an agent of genetic change.

Transverse connectives

The most advanced forms have the cords fused to form a single cord. A ganglionic swelling of the cord is found in each body segment, with the most anterior ganglion, the subpharyngeal ganglion, being the most prominent.

first found in helminths

Trichoblasts

A hairlike or bristlelike outgrowth, as from the epidermis of a plant.

Triplet code

A set of three-nucleotide-long words that specify the amino acids for polypeptide chains.

Trichomes

Extensions from the epidermis of the plant that provides shade and protection for the plant.

Triploblastic

Possessing three germ layers: the endoderm, mesoderm, and ectoderm. Most eumetazoans are triploblastic.

Trophic level

The division of species in an ecosystem based on their main nutritional source. The trophic level that ultimately supports all others consists of autotrophs or primary producers.

Trophic structure

The different feeding relationships in an ecosystem that determine the route of energy flow and the pattern of chemical cycling.

Trophoblast

The outer epithelium of the blastocyst, which forms the fetal part of the placenta.

Tropic

About behaviour or action brought about by specific stimuli, for example, phototropic ("light-oriented") motion, gonadotropic ("stimulating the gonads") hormone.

Tropic hormone

A hormone that has another endocrine gland as a target.

Tropical rain forest

The most complex of all communities, located near the equator where rainfall is abundant; harbours more species of plants and animals than all other terrestrial biomes combined.

Tropism

A growth response that results in the curvature of whole plant organs toward or away from stimuli due to differential rates of cell elongation.

Truncus arteriosus

An artery connected with the fetal heart, developing into the aortic and pulmonary arches. The trunk may persist into extrauterine life. The single arterial trunk from the heart supplies blood to both aortic and pulmonary circuits.

Tuatara

Either of two nocturnal lizardlike reptiles *(Sphenodon punctatus* or *S. guntheri)* that are found only on certain islands off New Zealand and are the only extant members of the Rhynchocephalia, an order that flourished during the Mesozoic Era. Also called *sphenodon.*

Tuber

A much-enlarged, short, fleshy underground stem, such as that of the potato.

Tuberous stem

Producing or bearing tubers.

Tubulin

The constituent protein of microtubules of cells which provide a skeleton for maintaining cell shape and is thought to be involved in cell motility.

Tumour

A mass that forms within otherwise normal tissue, caused by the uncontrolled growth of a transformed cell.

Tumour suppressor gene

A gene whose protein products inhibit cell division, thereby preventing uncontrolled cell growth (cancer).

Tundra

A biome at the extreme limits of plant growth; at the northernmost limits, it is called arctic tundra, and at high altitudes, where plant forms are limited to low shrubby or matlike vegetation, it is called alpine tundra.

Tunicates

Any of various sedentary tunicates of the class Ascidiacea, having a transparent sac-shaped body with two siphons. Also called *ascidian.*

Turgid

Firm; walled cells become turgid as a result of the entry of water from a hypotonic environment.

Turgor

The pressure exerted by fluid in a cell that presses the cell membrane against the cell wall.

Turgor pressure

The force-directed against a cell wall after the influx of water and the swelling of a walled cell due to osmosis.

Twisted

To interlock or interlace.

Tympanic

Relating to the middle ear or eardrum.

Tympanum

The main cavity of the ear, between the eardrum and the inner ear.

Tyrosine kinase

An enzyme that catalyzes the transfer of phosphate groups from ATP to the amino acid tyrosine in a substrate protein.

Tyrosine kinase receptor

A receptor protein in the plasma membrane that responds to the binding of a signal molecule by catalyzing the transfer of phosphate groups from ATP to tyrosines on the cytoplasmic side of the receptor. The phosphorylated tyrosines activate other signal- transduction proteins within the cell.

U

Ultimate causation

The hypothetical evolutionary explanation for the existence of a certain pattern of animal behaviour.

Ultrastructural View

The detailed structure of a biological specimen, such as a cell, tissue, or organ, that can be observed only by electron microscopy. Also called *fine structure*.

Unicellular

Having or consisting of one cell

Unicellular protozoans

Any of a large group of single-celled, usually microscopic, eukaryotic organisms, such as amoebas, ciliates, flagellates, and sporozoans.

Unisexual

Having only one type of sexual organ.

Unsaturated fatty acid

A fatty acid possessing one or more double bonds between the carbons in the hydrocarbon tail. Such bonding reduces the number of hydrogen atoms attached to the carbon skeleton.

Unreactive

Not reacting chemically.

Urea

A soluble form of nitrogenous waste excreted by mammals and most adult amphibians.

Urea cycle

The urea cycle is a cycle of biochemical reactions occurring in many animals that produces urea from ammonia (NH_3). This cycle was the first metabolic cycle discovered (Kerbs and Kurt Henseleit, 1932). In mammals, the urea cycle takes place only in the liver.

Ureter

A duct leading from the kidney to the urinary bladder.

Urethra

A tube that releases urine from the body near the vagina in females or through the penis in males; also serves in males as the exit tube for the reproductive system.

Uric acid

An insoluble precipitate of nitrogenous waste excreted by land snails, insects, birds, and some reptiles.

Urinary bladder

An elastic, muscular sac situated in the anterior part of the pelvic cavity in which urine collects before excretion.

Urine

The liquid waste filtered from the blood by the kidney and stored in the bladder pending elimination through the urethra.

Urochordate

A chordate without a backbone, commonly called a tunicate, a sessile marine animal.

Urostyle

An unsegmented bone representing several fused vertebrae and forming the posterior part of the vertebral column in Anura.

Uterus

A female reproductive organ where eggs are fertilized and/or development of the young occurs.

V

Vaccine

A harmless variant or derivative of a pathogen that stimulates a host's immune system to mount defences against the pathogen.

Vacuole

A membrane-enclosed sac taking up most of the interior of a mature plant cell and containing a variety of substances important in plant reproduction, growth, and development.

Vagina

Part of the female reproductive system between the uterus and the outside opening; the birth canal in mammals; also accommodates the male's penis and receives sperm during copulation.

Valence shell

The outermost energy shell of an atom, containing the valence electrons involved in the chemical reactions of that atom.

Valvate

Meeting at the edges without overlapping, as some petals do.

Van-der Waals interactions

Weak attractions between molecules or parts of molecules that are brought about by localized charge fluctuations.

Vaporization

The change from a liquid to a gas; evaporation.

Variation

Diversity among the members of a population. Variation among individuals can exist at many levels, including genetic, physiologic and behavioural.

Vas deferens

The tube in the male reproductive system in which sperm travel from the epididymis to the urethra.

Vascular

Containing or concerning vessels that conduct fluid.

Vascular bundle

In plants, a group of longitudinal supporting and conducting tissues (xylem and phloem).

Vascular cambium

A continuous cylinder of meristematic cells surrounding the xylem and pith that produces secondary xylem and phloem.

Vascular plants

Plants with vascular tissue, consisting of all modern species except the mosses and their relatives.

Vascular tissue

Plant tissue consisting of cells joined into tubes that transport water and nutrients throughout the plant body.

Vascular tissue system

A system formed by xylem and phloem throughout the plant, serving as a transport system for water and nutrients, respectively.

Vector

In recombinant DNA, a small, self-replicating DNA molecule, or a portion thereof, into which a DNA segment can be spliced and introduced into a cell; generally a plasmid or a virus.

Vegetative

Relating to or characteristic of plants or their growth.

Vegetative reproduction

Cloning of plants by asexual means.

Vein

A vessel that returns blood to the heart. Veins (from the Latin vena) are blood vessels that carry blood toward the heart.

Vena cava

A large vein that brings blood from the tissues to the right atrium of the four-chambered mammalian heart. The superior vena cava collects blood from the forelimbs, head, and anterior or upper trunk; the inferior vena cava collects blood from the posterior body region.

Ventilation

Any method of increasing contact between the respiratory medium and the respiratory surface.

Ventral

About the undersurface of an animal that holds its body in a horizontal position; to the front surface of an animal that holds its body erect.

Vernanimalcula

Vernanimalcula guizhouena is a fossil believed by some to represent the earliest known member of the Bilateria (animals with bilateral symmetry)

Ventricle

A muscular chamber of the heart that receives blood from an atrium and pumps blood out of the heart, either to the lungs or to the body tissues.

Venule

A very small vein. See also Vein.

Vorticella convellaria

Any of various protozoa having a transparent goblet-shaped body with a retractile stalk

Vertebral column

The backbone; in nearly all vertebrates, it forms the supporting axis of the body and protects the spinal cord.

Vertebrate

A chordate animal with a backbone: the mammals, birds, reptiles, amphibians, and various classes of fishes.

Vesicle

A small, intracellular membrane-bound sac.

Vessel element

A specialized short, wide cell in angiosperms; arranged end to end, they form continuous tubes for water transport.

Vestigial organ

A type of homologous structure that is rudimentary and of marginal or no use to the organism.

Vexillary

A member of the oldest class of army veterans who served under a special standard in ancient Rome.

Viable

Able to live.

Villus

In vertebrates, one of the minute, fingerlike projections lining the small intestine that serve to increase the absorptive surface area of the intestine.

Viroid

A plant pathogen composed of molecules of naked RNA only several hundred nucleotides long.

Virulent

Capable of overcoming a host's defence mechanisms and causing a disease sometimes of rapid onset and severe symptoms.

Virulence factors

Virulence factors are molecules produced by a pathogen that specifically influence their host's function to allow the pathogen to thrive.

Virus

A submicroscopic, noncellular particle composed of a nucleic acid core and a protein coat (capsid); parasitic; reproduces only within a host cell.

Viscera

The collective term for the internal organs of an animal.

Visceral muscle

Smooth muscle found in the walls of the digestive tract, bladder, arteries, and other internal organs.

Visible light

That portion of the electromagnetic spectrum detected as various colours by the human eye, ranging in wavelength from about 400 nm to about 700 nm.

Vitalism

The belief that natural phenomena are governed by a life force outside the realm of physical and chemical laws.

Vitamin

An organic molecule required in the diet in very small amounts; vitamins serve primarily as coenzymes or parts of coenzymes.

Vitellarium

A group of glands that secrete yolk around the egg in those invertebrates, such as worms, whose eggs do not contain yolk.

Viviparous

Referring to a type of development in which the young are born alive after having been nourished in the uterus by blood from the placenta.

Voltage-gated channel

Ion channel in a membrane that opens and closes in response to changes in membrane potential (voltage); the sodium and potassium channels of neurons are examples.

Vomerine

A thin trapezoidal bone of the skull forming the posterior and inferior parts of the nasal septum

Water cycle

Worldwide circulation of water molecules, powered by the sun. Water evaporates from oceans, lakes, rivers, and, in smaller amounts, soil surfaces and bodies of organisms; Water returns to the Earth in the form of rain and snow. Of the water falling on land, some flows into rivers that pour water back into the oceans and some percolates down through the soil until it reaches a zone where all pores and cracks in the rock are filled with water (groundwater); the deep groundwater eventually reaches the oceans, completing the cycle.

Water potential

The physical property predicting the direction in which water will flow, governed by solute concentration and applied pressure.

Water vascular system

A network of hydraulic canals unique to echinoderms that branches into extensions called tube feet, which function in locomotion, feeding, and gas exchange.

Wavelength

The distance between crests of waves, such as those of the electromagnetic spectrum.

Webbed

Connected by a membrane or strand of tissue.

Wild type

An individual with the normal phenotype.

Wobble

A violation of the base-pairing rules in that third nucleotide (5' end) of a tRNA anticodon can form hydrogen bonds with more than one kind of base in the third position (3' end) of a codon.

Worker

A member of the nonreproductive labouring caste of social insects.

Woroninan bodies

Woroninan bodies are cytoplasmic organelles which commonly lie near the septa in ascomycetous fungi.

X

Xerophytes

A plant adapted to living in a dry arid habitat; a desert plant.

A plant adapted for life with a limited supply of water; compare hydrophyte and mesophyte.

Xylem

The tube-shaped, nonliving portion of the vascular system in plants that carries water and minerals from the roots to the rest of the plant.

Xanthophyll

The yellow pigment in the plant that, like chlorophyll, is responsible for the production of carbohydrates by photosynthesis.

Y 

Yeast

A unicellular fungus that lives in liquid or moist habitats, primarily reproducing asexually by simple cell division or by budding of a parent cell.

Yolk

The stored food in egg cells that nourishes the embryo.

Yolk sac

One of four extraembryonic membranes that support embryonic development; the first site of blood cells and circulatory system function.

Z

Zoned reserve systems

Habitat areas that are protected from human alteration and surrounded by lands that are used and more extensively altered by human activity.

Zoology

The study of animals.

Zooplankton

A collective term for the nonphotosynthetic organisms present in plankton.

Zoospore

An asexual spore of some algae and fungi that moves using flagella.

Zwitterions

A molecule carrying both a positive and a negative charge.

Zygomorphic

Relating to a flower that can be divided into equal halves along only one line; bilaterally symmetrical. The flowers of the iris and the snapdragon are zygomorphic.

Zygospores

A large multinucleate spore formed by the union of similar gametes, as in algae or fungi. A plant spore formed by two similar sexual cells.

Zygote

The diploid product of the union of haploid gametes in conception; a fertilized egg.

Zygotene

The stage in prophase of meiosis during which homologous chromosomes become paired.

∞

The End